# Life and Education of Children in Nepal

(Pre and Post Peace Agreement a Comparative Study)

# Life and Education of Children in Nepal

(Pre and Post Peace Agreement a Comparative Study)

Shree Prasad Devkota

ADROIT
Adroit Publishers
New Delhi

ISBN : 978-81-87393-50-4

First Published in 2017



*Published by*
**ADROIT PUBLISHERS**
4675/21, Ganpati Bhawan, Ansari Road,
Daryaganj, New Delhi-110 002
Phone : 011-23266030

Exclusively Distributed by:

**Vijay Enterprises**
4675/21, Ganpati Bhawan,
Ansari Road, Daryaganj
New Delhi, INDIA
Mob.: +91-9899717865

*Typesetting – Gaurav Graphices, Delhi-110002*
*E-mail: gauravsingh1908@gmail.com*
*Printed at: Rajyoriya Prints, Delhi.*

# Dedicated to

*To*

*Those conflict affected children*

*Who are searching their future in the Post-Conflict Situation*

# Abstract


## Genesis of Cause

It has now become all apparent that the ten years long armed conflict in Nepal has caused school going children Severe mentally and physical pain: A barrier to their group and development. Considering this aspect, the present study proposes two research questions: (a) what did school children experience their education and life during the ten years long armed conflict? (b) how were they experienceing their life after the peace agreement?

To explore their experience, a phenomenological case study was carried out in Gorkha district with two male and two female children of aged under 18 during the 10 years armed conflict in Nepal. An in-depth interview was carried out and the information was analyzed by exploring the themes. Credibility was maintained through prolonged engagement in the field, thick description of the study context, sharing finding with the participants and conducting deliberation . To ensure the ethics, participants were fully assured or sapedy and pseudonyms were used where they desired.

The findings of the study show that several reasons like (i)extreme poverty, (ii) social exclusion, (iii) milien of discrimination, (iv) parental involvement in CPN (Maoist), parents' profession, and torture from both the state security forces and the CPN (Maoist); compelled the research participants to get affected by the conflict. As their parents used to get involved in armed-conflict, they had the responsibility to execise all household works and so to keep them away from formal education.

**So-called Support: Only Bail Like to Rule**

After the Peace Agreement, they were getting some sort of support from the government and different development organizations. However, the participants were not satisfied with the support that they were provided as it was insufficient for them for their sustainable livelihood. Along with the economic, derangement they were also facing psychological and social challenges. In addition, they suffered social exclusion one way or other. The findings also show that the education after the **peace agreement** had not been in their priority than that of taking care of their family members and sustainable livelihoods. However, there was a participant who continued his study in a very difficult situation.

**What's Need or Hour?**

This study concludes that there is an urgent need for victim-centred and individualized approaches rather than 'one size fits all' approach to address the need of conflict affected children. This kind of contextual practice directly addresses the local and individual needs. By this, the needs of the victims can be linked to their vocations for their sustainable future. It is hoped this book (alias research paper) will enable one and all understanding what real mean of "Peace" is And how is brought to each individual heart and also for a region territory stap cordially and the world as a whole.

**Some Quotaintion Anonymous**

*On Peace Agreement*

(i) Ruling ambition pierces the soul of peace.

(ii) When will society and its people understand today's

School going children will take revenge of what they are made to suffer?

(iii) To rule cannot bring peace perspective of condition and clauses in Agreements, its awareness and ideal alltude that can fetch an utopian piece and unanimous support.

# Acknowledgements

**Scope of Assignment /Project**

This research is presented in partial caireing to the requirements for my Master of Philosophy in Education at Kathmandu University School of Education.

The pursuit of this MPhil has been a long and arduous journey for me, involving several tasks to make my way through these three percerenant years of study. I am therefore indebted to several individuals who have contributed to this research. I am particularly grateful to my dissertation supervisor, **Asst. Prof. Dr. Prakash C Bhattarai** for all his support, genuine guidance and encouragement throughout this study his endear our contributed immensely to the completion of this work.

Similarly, I would like to express my heart felt gratitude to **Prof. Dr. Mahesh Nath Parajuli,** Dean of School of Education, and Kathmandu University for his contribution as continuous mentor during this research. It would have not been possible to bring the inquiry in this form but for, his timely encouragement and support. I am equally indebted to **Dr. Bal Chandra Luitel,** Associate Dean of Kathmandu University, School of Education, and **Prof. Dr. Mana Prasad Wagley** for his mindful suggestions all the way through. Likewise, I would like to express my gratitude to my friend **Rupa Munakarmi** and **Rebat Kumar Dhakal** for their support in bestowing fine tune and hormony to the entire dissertation with academic language and giving it shape as recommended by American Psychological Association's guidelines (6th edition).

**My Relations**

I am grateful to my father **Chudamani Devkota**, mother **Bhagabati Devkota**, brother **Bikash** and sisters **Radha** and **Laxmi** for their providing me continuous inspiration and escalation during the study. I am also thankful to my father -in-law Ram **Chandra Bagale** and mother -in-law **Satya Devi Bagale** for their kind support and encouragement. I am equally indebted to my sisters-in-law **Bindu Bagale** and **Anupama Bagale**.

In Similar Fashion, special thanks showed go to my dearest wife **Shiba Bagale** for her wonderful company, with whom I felt more confident and comfortable to win every race of my life. **Shiba** is a true friend and soul mate who shares my success on completion of this study.

Finally, I wish to express my gratitude to all men milieu, mechanism and mochrs - operandi, that have combined by contributed to this work directly or indirectly even though they remain anonymous and factors of intuition.

**Shree Prasad Devkota, M.Phil**

Here, at conclusion, what and when to communicates as below:

(i) Every aspect of life is interrelated all human beings are related to one - another and by harming another, they harm themselves and again.

(ii) Whatever action a greatman performs, common men follow, and - what ever standards, he sets by exemplary acts, all the world pursues the same.

# Contents

## Acronyms/Abbreviations Used in this Work

| | |
|---|---|
| AMMAA | Agreement on the Monitoring of the Management of Arms and Armies |
| ANNSU(R) | All Nepal National Independent Students Union (Revolutionary) |
| CAAC | Children Affected by Armed Conflict |
| CAAFAG | Children Associated with Armed Forces & Armed Groups |
| COID | Commission of Inquiry on Disappearances |
| CPA | Comprehensive Peace Agreement |
| CPN | Communist Party of Nepal |
| CRC | Convention on the Rights of the Child |
| CZOP | Children as a Zone of Peace |
| CREHPA | Centre for Research on Environment Health and Population Activities |
| DDC | District Development Community |
| DDR | Disarmament Demobilization and Reintegration |
| DFID | Department for International Development |

| | |
|---|---|
| GoN | Government of Nepal |
| INGOs | International Non-Governmental Organizations |
| ICESCR | International Covenant on Economic, Social and Cultural Rights |
| ICRC | International Committee of the Red Cross |
| IHRC | International Human Right Clinic |
| IHRICON | Institute of Human Rights Communication in Nepal |
| ILO | International Labor Organization |
| INSEC | Informal Sector Service Center |
| IRP | Interim Relief Program |
| MOPR | Ministry of Peace and Reconstruction |
| MOWCSF | Ministry of Women, Children and Social Welfare |
| NGO | Non-Governmental Organizations |
| NIPS | National Institute for Policy Studies |
| NPTF | Nepal Peace Trust Fund |
| PLA | People's Liberation Army |
| PPCAC | Partnerships for Protecting Children in Armed Conflict |
| SLC | School Leaving Certificate |
| SMCS | School management Committee |
| SPA | Seven-Party Alliance |
| SZOP | School as a Peace of Zone |
| TC | Truth Commission |

| | |
|---|---|
| TRC | Truth and Reconciliation Commission |
| UN CRC | United Nations Convention on the Rights of the Children |
| UN | United Nations |
| UNCF | United Nation Children Fund |
| UNDP | United Nation Development Program |
| UNEPA | United Nation Fund for Population Activities |
| UNESCO | United Nation Educational, Scientific and Cultural Organization |
| UNICEF | United Nation International Children's Emergency Fund |
| UNMIN | United Nation Mission in Nepal |
| VDC | Village Development Committee |

# 1

# Introduction

Nepal's Maoists - the Communist Party of Nepal (Maoist), the CPN (M) -launched an armed conflict in Nepal in 1996, which was then called the 'People's War' (see Gautam, 2006). It was started by the then revolutionary political party, the Communist Party of Nepal-Maoist (CPN-Maoist). The conflict continued for ten years until the CPN (Maoist) formally got into the peace agreement in 2006 with the political agenda of overthrowing the constitutional monarchy which was despotic and undemocratic. The prime motive of the war was to establish 'a new socio-economic structure and state of Nepal' with the inclusive representation of all socially excluded, marginalized and other back-warded people in the Nepali societies (Bhattarai, 2003).

According to Thapa (2003), "Nepal was a monolithic, feudalistic, autocratic, authoritarian, centralized and closed state for centuries" (as cited in Upreti, 2006, p. 24). He further states that the state governing system in the entire history of modern Nepal was orchestrated by cajoling, threat of suppression and use of coercive power by the state. Such characteristics of the state consequently excluded a vast majority of Nepali people from the nation-building process. This converted nearly an upbringing of insurgency in Nepal. Sharma (2006) also supports this argument. He states that the existing development policy initiated in 1980s of 'urban-based import substitution industrialization' led to the increase inequality, exclusion and stratification with the majority of people in Nepal. The gap between the poor and the rich increased as the development was focused on urban areas, by which consequently, rural people became poorer. Only some powerful people were in the ruling system and they were from the high class of the society so they did not respond to the problems of low class people in the society. In this way, the gap became wider, making poor, poorer and the rich richer. So the elites were getting all the fruits of development and poor, women and disadvantaged are . So the disadvantaged group (Dalit, socially excluded, ethnic community, marginalized) was backward in terms of education, health, social status, and politics. It has created a huge gap in the society on the basis of class, caste, ethnicity etc.

## Consearwrces of Gap in the Society

The gap in the society has created several problems. The poor are not getting even the basic needs whereas the rich have no any such problems. In order to to fulfill the gap, to create equality and equity in the society and to address the problems of those groups, the CPN (Maoist) started launching revolution against the government to fulfill their political aspirations . According to the CPN (Maoist) document, fundamentally; the war was to change the 'historical relations of oppression' in Nepal (K. L. Devkota, *personal communication, February 25, 2015*). On the base of the conflict in the society, the revolution was started in 1996 to address it. Therefore, especially youth from Dalit and other marginalized groups were encouraged and motivated because they realized that they were dominated and exploited by the despotic upper caste and government self. A , a number of youth from those communities, joined the radical left wing force, i.e. CPN (Maoist) to fight against the political system, social stratification/exclusion and economic policy of the country (Shakya, 2006). With some more clarifications, Neupane

(2003) stated that *the reason behind the involvement of the youths in the CPN* (Maoist) party was their social and political agendas which has addressed the unequal distribution of the power and the discrimination, social exclusion that they were facing around them. (So, the backwarded and people of remote areas were not satisfied with the existing system and the CPN (Maoist)'s pathway has captured their essence.)

## A Decade Long Conflict: Aspiratichs

The ten years long armed conflict was initiated with the help of many youths by the CPN (Maoist) party. The youths have dreamt a beautiful Nepal where there would not be any chaos, discrimination, poverty, domination and have fought with the passion *(L. M. Pokherel, personal communication, March 22, 2015)*. After ten years' time, the conflict ended with the twelve-point agreement between the revolutionary party – CPN (Maoist) and seven parties of the nation (Devkota, 2014). The revolution party and the government of Nepal have argued to turn the name "People's War" into "armed conflict" after the Comprehensive Peace Accord (CPA).

The conflict resulted in both negative and positive consequences in the society *(Shakya, 2006)*. Shakya further highlighted that the positive aspects of the conflict are: people are empowered, aware and are able to raise their voices. There has been (i) *an increase in awareness of human rights among Nepalese people* and (ii) *this armed conflict made people able to fight against social, cultural and political discrimination*. As per report from Ministry of Peace and Reconstruction (2013) 17,886 people lost their lives during the armed conflict and more than 1,300 still missing people (MoPR, 2013, as per report published in National Institute for Policy Studies, 2013). The armed conflict not only harmed the people but also destroyed physical infrastructures worth NRs. 5,000 million (equivalent to 71 million U.S. dollar) like many drinking water systems, tele communication towers, barracks, suspension bridges, government offices including village development committee offices and health posts neighboring to it and police posts (B. K., 2010).

The positive impacts have done good for the society while the negative impacts have created a trauma to the people affected. Pherali (2011) stated that from very young children to the old age, rural people to the urban, government officials to the laymen, all have severally suffered in one or the other way. Specially, the government organizations like schools, offices, hospitals etc. were the main targeted areas. The state security force had taken school as a barrack whereas the CPN (Maoist) parties had taken it as a place for conducting different political programs, meetings, etc. Though different international laws had announced school as zone of peace, the situation in the conflict time was different. Affecting or damage of schools and hospitals were/are banned under the well-established international humanitarian law: treaty and customary law, and that all is a violation of the rights of the child (United Nations [UN], 2013). Also the schools were closed, padlocked in different districts saying that the education was "*Bourgeois*" which was not in favor of the lower class people. And they focused on "*Janawadi shikshya*" (people centric education which includes all classes). Many teachers and students were killed in the crossfire between the CPN (Maoist) and the state forces. So it seemed that the schools were the battleground; not the peace zone as presumed only in worlds

The CPN (Maoist) party enforced teachers to pay certain levy (cash donation) and support their political ideology. Some of the teachers were also the followers of the CPN (Maoist) ideology and they left schools for some days to conduct different political programs. The teachers were not safe from both sides. Some were killed for providing information to the state security force and some were killed for being the CPN (Maoist) supporter.

Consequently, students were also forced to participate in different cultural programs organized by the CPN (Maoist) party. Some of them became the follower by knowing the political ideology but some of them got affected for not following them. Parents' involvement in CPN (Maoist) was also one of the causes on the student's involvement in the CPN (Maoist) party. So the situation during that period was very difficult for students to get formal education. In such circumstances, it had created fear among all the school children.

## Statement of the Research Problem

### *Efforts of Peace Make After Conflict*

After signing a Comprehensive Peace Accord (CPA) on 21 November, 2006 by both parties (State and CPN -Maoist), the decade long armed conflict was formally ended in Nepal. Then, both the signatories agreed to end all resentments, safeguard human rights and start making preparations for assimilating the CPN (Maoist) fighters into the Nepal Army and to provide some reliefs to the conflict affected. They also agreed to keep the CPN (Maoist) fighters temporarily in cantonment until they were integrated into the national army (see UN, 2011).

On the basis of the CPA, the Interim Constitution of Nepal, 2063 (2007 C.E.) was introduced and implemented. If we see the details about the conflict and its relief, in part three, it is given as providing proper assistance, recognition and rehabilitation of the families of those who were killed and for those persons being disabled and made helpless through injury caused by the walking or running through path of the armed conflict (Gautam, 2007). In the same way, the Interim Constitution further made a provision to provide relief to the families of the affected on the basis of the report of the Investigation Commission instituted to explore the cases of persons who were the subject of imposed disappearance during the course of the conflict (refer to Government of Nepal [GoN], 2007). Similarly, different NGOs and civil society run many other initiatives to socialize and rehabilitate the conflict affected children in their society, rejoin their education give effect to and reintegration in their society.

As mentioned in the CPA, the GoN has adopted a National Plan of Action and various programs for the rehabilitation and reintegration of Children affected by Armed Conflict. The relief programs were self-retirement of the ex-combatants, compensation to families of the deceased ones, scholarship for the children who were under the age of 18 (GoN, 2012). It yielded somehow positive results; as some children were able to continue to be educated on a daily basis (refer to Farasat & Hayner, 2009).

## *Reforms for Name-Sake*

Nevertheless, the significant progress has not been seen in the number of children enrolling in school and higher education after the ceasefire even though the government and some organizations conducted different support programs. According to Devkota (2015), whatever programs have been initiated, they are still suffering from its effects, thoroughly different; the families of the dead can mourn and gradually, rebuild their lives with many obstacles. Similarly, for the families of the missing, there is no end to their pain: sons, husbands, wives and daughters are disappeared, taken away by either party of the conflict, and their families are still waiting to know their whereabouts.

## *Pireous Condition of Conflict Affected Children*

The school children were seen physically as well as mentally affected in the post-conflict situation. Regarding this, a report namely, Upreti and Boker (2010) also states that conflict affected children are facing difficulty in socializing in their society because of losing their academic life in conflict, losing their parents and other relatives in conflict, etc. So it is necessary to explore the better relief and assistance package programs for those children to address the impact of conflict with a long term vision. Pradhan (2012) also focused on different stresses and poverty which have been the obstacles for them to live a normal life. Moreover, Wessells (1998) also highlighted that the conflict affected children are having the problems of aggression and change in the attitudes and have lost hope of life. It seems that the children in the post conflict situation are facing different sociological, physical and mental problems of reintegration in the society.

### *Special Needs of Conflict Affected Children*

Thus, it is necessary to identify the special needs of the conflict affected children in the post conflict situation to implement suitable programs for their empowerment and social, mental reintegration in the society. To cite an example, after the peace agreement in Sri Lanka, the children are provided with different education, psychological programs, social awareness programs and facilities for the livelihood (EU, 2010, as cited in Pradhan, 2012). This helped them in reintegration in the society and for the livelihood, (i) in this view of issue so none of the affected was different from the non-affected children in the society. Pradhan (2012) further highlighted different vocational trainings, educations, counseling to provide to these children in Nepal as were provided in Sri Lanka. So it can be learnt that it is necessary to conduct such programs – providing psycho-social counseling, social rehabilitation and social re-integration as well as skill-oriented and self-employment programs keeping in mind their interest, ability, needs and market prospects for rebuilding their lives – in the post conflict situation.

## Purpose of the Study

The purpose of this study is to explore how the school going children have experienced their education and life during the decade long armed conflict. (supra) Furthermore, it aims to highlight their experi and its conversion in good for their life after the peace agreement.

## Research Questions

The main research question of the study is: pro and post conflict experience of school going children about their education and life in Nepal? Similarly, the sub-questions derived out of the main research questions are the following:

1. What was the experience is the school children had about their education and life during that dacade long armed conflict ?
2. How are these conflict affected children experiencing their life after above said peace agreement?

## Significance of the Study

As a researcher, I have raised the issue of the experiences of the conflict affected school children, especially; their education during the ten years long armed conflict in Nepal. The education during the conflict and at present situation, has a great significance for this researcher and for the society as well that which helps to know about the real scenario of education; about how the academic career is severly damaged by the conflict and the present life of the conflict affected and left as illiterate children in absence of education.

## The Research of Information: A Strong Factor

Firstly, it has been a good reservoir of information for me to understand the exact situation of the conflict as my schooling was also during the era of the conflict. I had heard some rumors of the conflict but this study has been helpful for me to understand how the education of the conflict affected children was and how they are making their living after peace agreement. This study would be helpful for the people who want to know the reality about how the children were compelled to be affected by the conflict. Also it would be helpful for the educators who really want to know the educational status of the conflict affected children and the educational needs after the peace agreement. This study would also become a cause of inspiration for policy makers, who really could add some policies to address the issues of conflict affected children in Nepal. It would also be a good lesson to the conflict experts nationally and internationally to know the way of conflict that the children faced and the strategies of conflict resolution through the peace agreement.

# 2

# Literature Review

## What Dwells Inside?

In this chapter, I have reviewed different relevant literatures. It consists of the thematic review, empirical review, policy review and theoretical reviews based on the experiences of the children on education during and post conflict situations. I started my expedition on the literature based on the periphery of these terms. I went through various books, journals, previous researches, on-line articles, digital thesis etc. that provided me with the context and ideas for the design of my research. In this chapter, I have presented my ideas thematically, and critically. I claim such kind of review 'an atomic review' because it provides a powerful technique to understand the required field in a greater detail.

## Conflict: An Introduction

Conflict refers to the disagreement between persons, individuals, groups or societies. Warner (2001) defines conflict as, "a debate or contest; a disagreement, argument, dispute, quarrel; a struggle, battle or confrontation; or a state of unrest, turmoil, chaos and violence" (as cited in Upreti, 2006, p. 54). There are several reasons where conflict starts. Upreti (2006) quotes; "Conflict occurs when two or more people oppose one another because of the difference in their needs, wants, goals or values" (p. 54). Also, Handy (1983) defined conflict as "the process that begins when one party perceives that the other party frustrated or is about to frustrate some concern of his or her" (as cited in Ntiyakunze, 2011, p. 17).

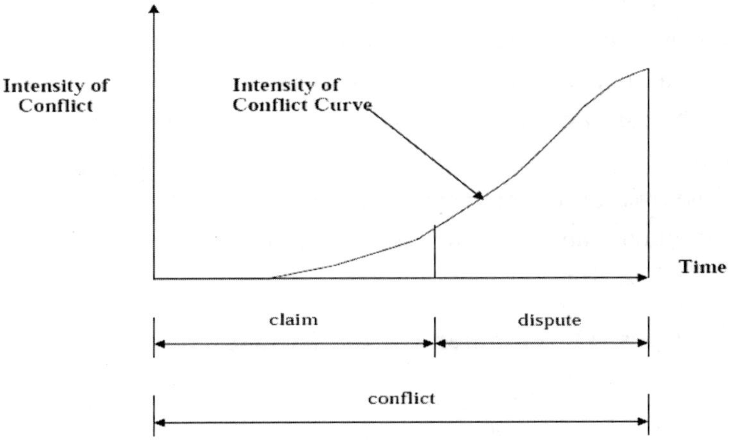


*Figure 1*: **The Spectrum of Conflict (Yates & Hardcastel, 2003, as cited in Ntiyakunze, 2011).**

The above figure also Clarifies how the conflict starts when the claim is untrue or false. That means conflict starts from the statement of a claim at one conclusion of the field to resolution of a disagreement at the other. "The increasing strength in the above curve is intensity of the conflict and intensity of feeling between the parties as the conflict receives progress through the various stages of a claim, which if unresolved;, develops into a dispute and proceeds through the various resolution stages until it is ultimately resolved" (Yates & Hardcastel, 2003, as cited in Ntiyakunze, 2011, p. 18). So the conflict starts from the same point and time where the dispute increases. We experienced similar case in the starting of the conflict in Nepal back in 1996.

## Maoist Rebellion in Nepal: Defined

**Murshed and Gates** (2005) find that "horizontal inequalities in Nepal robustly explain the intensity of the CPN (Maoist) rebellion" (p. 3). But Do and Iyer (2009), on the other hand, have different reasons behind conflict. They do claim that the geography and poverty were the root causes of the conflict- not horizontal group inequality. So, there are different analytical perspectives on how conflict started in Nepal. In this, Upreti (2006) claimed that the prevailing structure of governance verified incapable to address the key issues like the corruption, improper service delivery and the inequitable rules and regulations, laws has forced to start conflict.

## Historical Development of the Armed Conflict

The word 'conflict' refers to the disagreement on different power, resources and posts. If we see the history of Nepal, there have been conflicts in different era for different purposes and many have lost the life, that the conflicts often involved destruction of other resources as well. But the armed conflict was a bit serious matter. It started due to the disagreement of the Communist Party of Nepal (Maoist) with the state and government. According to Thapa (2003), "Nepal was a monolithic, feudalistic, autocratic, authoritarian, centralized and closed state for centuries" (p. 24, as cited in Upreti, 2006). Furthermore he added that, "the state governing system in the entire history of modern Nepal was orchestrated by cajoling, threat of suppression and use of coercive power by the state. Such characteristics of the state consequently excluded a vast majority of the Nepali people from the nation-building process" (p. 24).Owing to that, this government system became upbringing ground of revolution in Nepal. Sharma (2006) also supports this agreement. He states that the current development policy started in 1980s of 'urban-based import substitution industrialization' has directly influenced to uplift the inequality in the society, extreme exclusion and crisis, discrimination was among the people within the country.

## Conflict in Nepal

The above discussion shows that the armed conflict in Nepal was because of the disagreement with the state's ruling parties who have not addressed the needs of the lower class people (Shakya, 2006). the party in the parliament has felt the domination and discrimination and planned in a different way to rebuild the nation. Human Rights Watch (n.d.) also reflects; People's war: now name to conflict "Parliament's dissolution of the communist government in 1995 helped spark the CPN (Maoist's) "People's War," an insurgency seeking to abolish the monarchy and re-establish communist rule" (as cited in International Human Rights Clinic [IHRC], 2013, p. 23). It was started on November 1995, by the CPN (Maoist) party by declaring it as the "people's war", where the CPN (Maoist) started the operation Romeo in Rolpa (K. L. Devkota, 10 February, 2015, personal communication). The armed conflict first initiated on 13 February 1996 by Communist Party of Nepal (Maoist) [CPN (M)] as a small insurgence in the four western hill districts of Nepal (K. L. Devkota, personal communication, August 25, 2015) and after that, it quickly expanded all over the country and posed several risks and danger on the security of the people in the whole country (Upreti, 2004).

During the conflict, many people lost their lives, many got disappeared, many injured. Likewise, many schools, hospitals, government offices, etc. were destroyed. According to the report of Informal Sector Service Centre [INSEC], a leading human rights organization of Nepal, *a total of 13,347 people died in the course of armed conflict from 1996 to 2006*. Similarly, other studies have reported that the armed conflict in Nepal has left a legacy of some

17,886 people lost their lives during the armed conflict (NIPS, 2013) and more than 1,300 are still missing (INSEC, 2007, as cited in Shakya, 2006, p. 8). This shows that different agencies have different data and due to lack of exact we cannot say the exact number of killed, disappeared and affected peoples of ten years armed conflict. In November 21, 2006, Nepal has got a way out from the armed conflict by signing on the CPA by the government (Seven Party Alliance, SPA) and CPN (M) (Upreti, 2008).

## Execution of Formal Document or Peace Agreement

The ten years' armed conflict could formally ended and the peace agreement began. It aimed to provide justice to the affected people and punishment to the criminals. So the CPA is the main formal document of the peace agreement

## International Commitments, Conferences and Declaration

There are different rules, regulations, laws and protocols to address the issues of rights of the children during the conflict. Many efforts were introduced for the protection of children right and their development afterward the First World War and at the beginning of the 1920s. Different organization had started their work on advocating and protection of children. Among them, 'Save the Children' issued the Five-Point Declaration on the Welfare and Development of Children in 1923. Likewise, significant declarations and world conferences were committed to protect children's rights and protection like, Declaration on the Rights of Children 1924; Universal Declaration of Human Rights 1948; Declaration on the Rights of the Child 1959; and the International Year of the Child 1979 etc.

## Role of UNO

Similarly, United Nation General Assembly named a special session on children and adopted the Convention on the Rights of the Child on 20 November, 1989 and that assembly espoused the action plan, "First Call for Children. Two Optional Protocols to the CRC—'Against the Sale of Children, Child Prostitution and Child Pornography' and 'Against the Use of Children in Armed Conflict'—were adopted in 2000" (MoPR & Mowcsw, 2010, p. 10). "The 1989 Convention on the Rights of the Child (CRC) is legally binding on all members of the United Nations, excluding Somalia and the United States of America as they have not ratified the Convention" (Catherine et al., 2008, p. 8). CRC has further described some child rights related policies .In the article 1 and article 4 of CRC, there is a clear rule mentioning for states parties and armed groups. According to this article, the state parties are responsible for the measures to be taken for the armed force who are under the age of 18. Similarly, this article also highlights that any armed group couldn't use or recruit children in any circumstances. It is taken as one of the most important international legal instruments for the child rights and their protection in the conflict and post conflict situation.

## UNO's Declaration on Child Right

Likewise, UN general assembly held another important session on child right and also adopted the declaration "A World Fit for Children". According to that declaration, the state parties need to promote the rights of the child and pay particular attention to a child's healthy life and the provision of free and compulsory basic primary education, including quality education; to the elimination of abuse, exploitation and violence against children; and to the introduction of campaigns against HIV and AIDS. State parties were also implored to develop a 10-Year long action plan. Plan of

Action. Nepal's 10-Year Plan of Action 2004–2014 was drawn up in 2004, and is currently being implemented (MoPR & Mowcsw, 2010, p. 10).

## UNO's Meetings

In 1997, UNICEF organized a meeting in Cape Town which adapted the Cape Town Principle. Specifically Cape Town Principle had addressed the problems and issues of Children affected by armed conflict (CAAC). Another, the Paris Commitments is taken as an important commitment to Protect Children Unlawfully Recruited or Used by Armed Forces or Armed Groups. Another complementary document which incorporated the principles and guidelines on Children related with Armed Forces or Armed Groups (The Paris Principles) were ratified by a ministerial level meeting in Paris in February, 2007.

## The Paris Principles

The Paris Principles, endorsed by 95 countries in 2010, focus on the "protection of the children in armed conflict" (Doek, 2011, p. 9). It highlights the stoppage of illegal recruitment or use of children. Furthermore, it deals with the release and reintegration of the child soldiers and children who have been involved in the conflict. Similarly, United Nations General Assembly 1974 has also adopted the Declaration of the security and protection of Women and Children in Emergency and Armed Conflict (Nilsson, 2005). It focused on children and women as they are the vulnerable groups in the conflict and their rights should be protected (Harvey, 2001). In this way, the vulnerable groups (Supra) affected of the conflict are given more priority. Equally, the rights of the children who are under age are protected differently.

## Responsibility of Said Parties to UNO

According to Harvey (2001), the responsibility and accountability of the State parties and the government to save the children in armed conflict are very fundamental and crucial. So the reports and conventions highlight specifically on the protection of child rights during the armed conflict and the state should bear the responsibility.

## National Commitment, Policy and Provision

Nepal's Status:- Nepal is a State Party to the International Bill of Rights and many international human rights laws including the International Covenant on Economic, Social and Cultural Rights (ICESCR, 1966) and the Convention on the Rights of the Child (UN CRC, 1989) as well. It has also ratified the Optional Protocol to the CRC on the Involvement of Children in Armed Conflict 2000.The Right to education as mentioned in articles 13 and 14 of the ICESCR and in article 27 of the UNCRC made states obliged and accountable for availability and accessibility to quality education along with equality for all school-aged children in Nepal without any discrimination (ICG, 2011). Therefore, it has expressed its commitment at the international level to comprehend and protect the rights of children. In this regard, it has developed and applied 10-Year Plan of Action for protection of children (2004–2014).

## Avowed AIMS of Ruling Parties

After the CPA, both parties (CPN -Maoist and Government) are committed to respect the international conventions and other protocol which are advocating ensuring the protection of children in the armed conflict and providing the necessary program to those children and other people who were affected in the ten years armed conflict. Similarly, through the Interim Constitution of Nepal, the government has enacted various laws and policies to ensure its commitment to the right to education and address the conflict affected students, helpless, orphaned or mentally retarded children, displaced, at risk and street children, highlighting that they shall have the right to receive special privileges from the State to ensure their secure future (as cited in CRC Reporting Coalition 2014, p. 38).

## Right to Education

The state's commitment to the right to education in Nepal has been evidenced in the Interim Constitution of Nepal, the School Sector Reform Plan, the National Plan of Action for Children, the three years Development Approach Paper and the engagement of civil society and the private sector in enhancing accessibility and quality of school education system with inclusive participation of all the people of the society. Similarly, the Interim Constitution of Nepal (2007) advocated that "the government should provide relief to the families of the affected who were subjected to disappearance during the course of armed conflict based on the report of the inquiry commission constituted in relation to such persons" (p. 17).

## Relief to Affected Families: of a Decade Long Conflict

Likewise, there is a strong commitment of both sides (State and CPN-Maoist) to provide the relief to the families of the affected both in CPA and the Interim Constitution of Nepal (2007). It was also mentioned to constitute the high-level Truth and Reconciliation Commission to investigate the truths about those persons involved in serious ruins of human rights and crimes against compassion committed during the period of the ten years' armed conflict, to create an atmosphere of settlement in the society who is really deprived due to the ten years armed conflict.

## Different Reality: Schools as Targets

### *Schools and School Going Children Suffered*

Schools across the conflict zones suffered the most during the conflict. From 1996-2006, Nepal agonized from armed conflict. Schools and education were gravely affected by this conflict: children were recruited into armed groups over the school yard, CPN (Maoist) party used schools for their own political ends, and School Management Committees (SMCs) were often unable to function properly due to intimidation of both party(CPN –Maoist and state security force) or instability. According to Education Journalists' Group, Nepal (n.d.), "the CPN (Maoist) has even threatened the school custodians to stop the government education system from functioning (accusing the education to be bourgeois) and pressurized to implement the 'Janawadi Sikchhaya' – the CPN (Maoist) curriculum" (p. 6). Moreover, teachers were also killed for ignoring the CPN (Maoist) intimidations. The teachers were teaching in the threatened environment with the news of the destruction of the schools and kidnapping and deaths of both the teachers and students.

### *Teachers Refused to Join Schools Under Fear*

While the government had announced to recruit new teachers but the fear of the conflict had intimidated the candidates to apply in the teacher vacancies and join their duty in the districts affected by the conflict. In such a situation, how could the children get education and perform better? It means teachers and students alike suffered from psychological pressure to keep themselves safe from the two forces. Thus, Joshi and Paudel (2006) state that school going children became the sufferers of the two political conflicts and they are still affected even in post conflict situation. At that time, the students and schools were in between both parties. Neither teacher were getting good environment to teach nor student were able to attain school. So education in Nepal has been under a serious tumult.

## *Red. Tapism: Gross Suppression*

Similarly, government security forces also made their temporary barracks near school and some were inside the schools. According to Gautam (2007), "Some schools had been occupied by the security forces in various parts of the country, such as Khotang, Myagdi, Syangja, Tanahu, Bara, Kathmandu, Rukum, Banke and Sindhuli districts" (p. 54). Since the April, 2006 cease-fire, most of the facilities occupied by the national army were vacated. Mostly school from the rural areas were used as battlegrounds and camps by both the parties, both parties attacked against schools and hospitals and school children are deprived of the humanitarian access (Pradhan, 2012) . The headlines in the media during the time of conflict were regarding blast of bombs, dozens killed, hundreds injured, school closed, exams cancelled etc.

## *Teachers and Students Under Pressure*

Teachers and students alike were under immense psychological pressure to keep them safe between two forces crossfire. "Scenes of bombs going off near their school, attack on school bus, burning of tires in the streets and dead bodies shown in TV channels on a regular basis - has tremendous psychological torture on student and teacher" (Education Journalists' Group, n.d., p. 7). During that time, either the CPN (Maoist) cadres or the members from the state security force were seen in the school yard. In such a situation, how can the children perform better? So the schools seemed to be the battlegrounds. How can we think that student could get right to education and teacher could teach in such circumstances?

### *Parents Under Suppression: Fear of Children in Climax*

Correspondingly, there was fear in the parents to send their children to schools. The parents had to be worried until their children returned back home from school. And the children were also in fear on the way or in the school because of the abduction by the CPN (Maoist) party and torture by the states security forces including sexual violence to female students. Neither the state nor the school committee was able to solve the problems that had affected the students. So, parents might choose not to send their children to school with a fear that they would be subject to the recruitment practices of the CPN (Maoist) and the potential abuse of the police.

### *Teaching Institutes: Not Accepted as Xones of Peace*

It was said that the ten years armed conflict did not explode due to education but it turned out to affect education sector the most. Both the state and the CPN (Maoist) failed to respect the universal values of human rights, and to accept educational institutes as zones of peace though national and international organizations, including the United Nations, endure to press for the same (Dhungana, 2006). So, school and education were affected in one or another way during the conflict, putting education under serious predicament. So thinking the interplay between education and conflict, we can analyse the nexus of the 'ten years' armed conflict' and education in Nepal and also can show how education served indirectly as one of the main causes of the violent conflict.

### *Different Reality: Student as Target*

The decade-long armed conflict ended after the Government of Nepal and the then Communist Party of Nepal (Maoist) signed the CPA on 21 November, 2006, (MoPR & Mowcsw, 2010). The country wriggled extensive loss of human life and property during the period of the armed conflict. It affected the all aged people's livelihood during the period of armed conflict and after the peace agreement.

School children were facing extreme negative Education of school going children: worst affected impacts because of ten years armed conflict. However, the actual statistics on conflict affected children are yet to be definite due to the changeable political situation and unstable government in the country .We can find some data on CAAC and CAAFAG which were provided by some organization, development partners and report. According to The National Human Rights Commission Report (2005), "500 children lost their lives, approximately 40,000 children were displaced, hundreds of children were wounded, and more than 8,000 children were orphaned or separated from their families in the course of the armed conflict since February, 1996" (as cited in MoPR & Mowcsw, 2010, p. 11).

### *Piteous Condition or Children Reported*

Similarly, Central Child Welfare Board (2009) stated that "Information received from 53 districts suggests that there are at least 19,980 CAAC. Of this figure, almost 50 percent (9,691 children) have been displaced with their parents and almost 20 percent (3,930 children) have lost either their mother or father" (as cited in MoPR & Mowcsw, 2010, p. 11). The report restated that 1,657 children have lost both parents and 671 have been disabled during the period of ten years armed conflict .Furthermore, this report highlighted that the number of children with one parent disappeared is 671 and with both parents disappeared is 149. Parents of 96 children have been disabled. The condition of almost 14 per cent of CAAC is unclear, (MoPR & Mowcsw, 2010, p. 11). Similarly, the records of the Task Force, which was made by the Ministry of Peace and Reconstruction to gather information on individuals, families and structures affected by the armed conflict, presented that over 78,600 people were recorded as displaced to mid-June 2010. However, the number of displaced children is not available till now.

### *School Going Children Used by Maoist*

Not only killed and displaced, the school children during the period of armed conflict were also used as per the need of both sides (CPN –Maoist and state security force). According to Gautam (2007), both the State and the CPN (Maoist) had used and affected the school going children, recruited the children as a fighter, cook, message taker, porter etc. even those children were under 18 years. During the period that decade long armed conflict, the rights of the people, especially children were ignored (Shakya, 2006). It means, children were used in the armed conflict in Nepal, ignoring the child convention and other child protection rules. They used them as their protective measure rather than protecting them from the armed conflict. Shakya further highlights that CPN (Maoist) party recruited children somewhere enforced and pressured, or duped children into joining armed conflict and state security force also charged the children as a CPN (Maoist) supporter and tortured regularly even in school going time during that decade long conflict in Nepal. .

### *Forced Children to Fight in Conflict*

Not only the forceful recruit of the children was the reason, there were other several reasons of involving children in the armed conflict. Further, Neupane (2003) emphasized that the social and political agenda of the CPN (Maoist) and the unsatisfactory circumstances that surrounded them motivated young people to get involved in the armed conflict even though they were below 18 years. And they joined CPN (Maoist) party without explicit coercion, although their decisions could not be regarded as voluntary because they were nearly always bounded by desperation and survival needs; so this situation lead them to get involved in the armed conflict (Shakya, 2006). It means, voluntary participation being motivated by the agenda was one factor whereas the family problems and parents were the other reasons.

### *Children who Post Parents*

As argued by Bhattachan and Webster (2005), some children were enforced to get captivated in the armed conflict because of the lost of their parents due to conflict. These conditions forced them to leave their academic career and get involved in the armed conflict. Among them, some were recruited as combatants and some were recruited as cooks, laborers and messengers (Gautam, 2007). On the other hand, the armed conflict was fatal to the livelihood of the children,

### *Outline of Children's Involvement in Conflict*

Most children were killed in the armed conflict, some remained injured, some uprooted from their homes and communities, some internally displaced or became refugees, orphans or got separated from their parents and relations (Pherali, 2011). They were mentally and physically traumatized as a result of being exposed to the violence. They were also deprived of their rights like health, education etc. and were neither protected by the state nor by any revolutionary party.

### *Harms to Children Caused by State Security Force*

Similarly, the state security force also harmed and affected the school children. According to Gautam (2007), the government security person constantly stressed and harassed the students for supporting

CPN (Maoist) party and sheltering them overnights and providing food to. It charged children as CPN (Maoist) supporters and also accused them to be the CPN (Maoist) activists, and thus, detained and subjected them to ill treatment and even torture practiced during interrogations (Pradhan, 2012). And there has been a widespread pattern of losses by security forces, including children under the age of 18, as part of the government's counterinsurgency operations (Gautam, 2007).

### *Several Reasons of Atrocity on Children*

On one hand, the school going children were tortured as their parent were involved in political parties other than the CPN (Maoist). On the other hand, the children whose parents were involved in or supported the CPN (Maoist) party were being tortured by the security forces. This way most of the children were affected during the conflict. Likewise, CPN (Maoist) abducted students for their political benefit and they also took forceful donations from teachers as a *levi* and membership charge from the students and they involved the students by force, in their political indoctrination and rallies.

### *Governments Lackadaisical Approach*

According to the International Committee of the Red Cross (ICRC) (2008, as cited ICG, 2011), governments must take the responsibility and should take steps to stop children being taken out of their own country illegally. Nevertheless, the government of Nepal is not obliged to take all needed steps to ensure that the minimum standards set by the convention in these areas are being met what mentioned on Article 11" (p. 8). In contrast, Gautam (2007) disagrees on the government role as kidnapping of the school going children by blaming them as the messengers of the CPN (Maoist) party and forced them to show their parents where they were hiding accusing their parents to be CPN (Maoist) fighters.

## Autocracy in Vogue Everywhere

It seemed that the conventions and protocols were only limited in the policies and were largely ignored during the conflict time in Nepal. The rebel party CPN (Maoist) also recruited the children in their forces by showing the inequality, social exclusion and injustice in their society and some of the children were attracted to get involved by the CPN (Maoist) political agenda of socially excluded and marginalized people (Upreti, 2006). So, it can be said that neither the government nor the CPN (Maoist) party were seen to have followed and implemented the child conventions. The children felt insecure and thus many of them were forced to leave their school and joined the armed conflict. Hence, whatever the child convention had mentioned most of the rules and regulations were broken during the ten years armed conflict in Nepal.

## Provisions of Law Worth Perusal

Additionally, articles 37 and 40 of the CRC are of particular importance for children in conflict. As mentioned in the Ministry of Women, Children and Social Welfare document (2012), it states that article 37 of CRC contains guarantees for children deprived of their liberty and their future life and their protection, and article 40 contains specific provisions concerning young justice while they were affected.

## All Conventions Declarations and Laws Violated

Whatever the principles are advocated by the Universal Declaration on Human Rights, the Convention on the Rights of the Child, the Geneva Conventions and other international humanitarian and human rights law, all those conventions and laws were busted in the ten years conflict of Nepal from the both sides (the State and the CPN (Maoist) . This was also reported by Amnesty International

(2005) as Nepalese children were denied their human rights, including for instance, their right to education. Not only this, the children were killed in the insurgence, many of them are still disappeared, being punished without respecting their human rights and even they are deprived from their basic rights along with several forms of violence.

## After Conflict, State Became Autocratic

Not only during the armed conflict but after the peace agreement as well, children have been facing several challenges due to the fact that the state did not follow the conventions. In the post conflict situation, some are still physically handicapped and psychologically traumatized and they are seen vulnerable and like urchin. They are helpless and neither the government nor the CPN (Maoist) party bothered to care them (United Nations Development Program [UNDP], 2014), which is contradictory of the declaration of the rights of the child principle of article number 5. It advocates that the child who is physically, mentally or socially handicapped shall be given the special treatment, education and care required by his particular condition and state has the main responsibility for this.

## Orphans and Desired Children Neglected

The article number 39 of CRC (as cited in Ministry of Peace and Reconstruction (2011) for rehabilitation of child affected states "children who have been neglected, abused or exploited should receive special help to physically and psychologically recover and reintegrate into the society" (p. 2). But here is a different reality from the above presented rules and regulation to protect the children. After losing the breadwinner of their family, children have been orphans, and are deprived of their rights. They are searching the secure way of living. They have thus the first priority to live rather than to get an education.

## No Changes in Children Condition Till Date

Therefore, it can be said that whatever human rights and child conventions advocate, the children are still suffering physically and mentally from the armed conflict they have endured. They are deprived of their right to live, education and other basic needs. That means they have an abysmal situation. It seems that child convention and other children protection rules are limited in slogan. So it is essential that the government of Nepal has to pay particular attention in restoring the health, education and other right of those conflict affected children as soon as possible.

## National Commitments, Policies and Programs

Nepal is a State Party to the International Bill of Rights and many international human rights laws including the International Covenant on Economic, Social and Cultural Rights (ICESCR, 1966) and the Convention on the Rights of the Child (UN CRC, 1989) as well. The Right to education as mentioned in articles 13 and 14 of the ICESCR and in article 27 of the UNCRC made states obliged and accountable for availability and accessibility to quality education along with equality for all school-aged children in Nepal without any discrimination and violence (UN, 2013).

## Extracts of Report by CRC Csalition

After the CPA, both parties (CPN -Maoist and Government) are committed to respect the international conventions and other protocol which are advocating ensuring the protection of children in the armed conflict and providing the necessary program to those children and other people who were affected in ten years armed conflict. Similarly, through the Interim Constitution of Nepal, the government has enacted various laws and policies to ensure its commitment to the right to education and address the conflict affected students, helpless, orphaned or mentally retarded children, displaced, at risk and street children, highlighting that they shall have the right to receive special privileges from the State to ensure their secure future (as cited in CRC Reporting Coalition, 2014, p. 38).

## State's Commitment to Right of Education

The state's commitment to the right to education in Nepal has been evidenced in the Interim Constitution of Nepal, the School Sector Reform Plan, the National Plan of Action for Children, the three years Development Approach Paper and the engagement of civil society and private sector in enhancing accessibility and quality of school education system with inclusive participation of all people of the society. Similarly, the Interim Constitution of Nepal (2007) advocates "the government should provide relief to the families of the affected who were subjected to disappearance during the course of armed conflict based on the report of the inquiry commission constituted in relation to such persons" (p. 17).

## A Joint Commitment: State and CPN. Maoist

Likewise, there is a strong commitment of both sides (State and CPN -Maoist) to provide the relief to the families of the affected in CPA and the Interim Constitution of Nepal (2007). As per the provision of CPA and the Interim Constitution of Nepal (2007):

Investigation Commission constituted to investigate the cases of persons who were subject to forceful disappearance during the course of the conflict, to conduct special program to rehabilitate the displaced persons, to provide compensation for damaged private and public property, and to rebuild infrastructure destroyed during the course of the conflict. (Cited in Ministry of Women, Children and Social Welfare, 2012)

## A Broad Picture of Commitments

It is also mentioned to constitute the high-level Truth and Reconciliation Commission to investigate the truths about those persons involved in serious ruins of human rights and crimes against compassion committed during the period of the ten years armed conflict, to create an atmosphere of settlement in the society who is really deprived due to the ten years armed conflict. Some commitments, efforts, policy and programs between government of Nepal, CPN (Maoist) and development related organizations are presented below.

## Ceasefire Code of Conduct

"CPN (Maoist) and the Seven-Party Alliance signed a 12-points understanding on 22 November, 2005 with the objective of establishing democracy in the country", (Ministry of Peace and Reconstruction, 2011, p. 13). As per this considerate, a 19-day's People's Movement enlarged ground resulting in reinstating the dissolved House of Representatives [the lower house of Parliament] on 24 April, 2006 (MoPR, 2011). Furthermore, MoPR reasserts that a ceasefire was then declared with the then CPN (Maoist) and the Government of Nepal signing a ceasefire code of conduct. The ceasefire code of conduct was agreed between the Government of Nepal and the CPN (Maoist) on 25 May, 2006. It has six different parts and divided into seven different points. They are: guaranteeing fearless civilian life, creating an environment of trust among the people, cooperation from media for peace talks, release and rehabilitation, facilitating the talks, monitoring and miscellaneous [Government of Nepal (GoN), 2006]. All the points are focused on the peace formation and ending of the 10 years armed conflict. Among them, some of the points are more relevant in terms of the affected and disappeared ones who were the parts of ten years armed conflict. Among them, Release and Rehabilitation consists of:

- Accusation, claims or cases filed by both the parties against various individuals will be withdrawn and the detainees will be released gradually.
- Whereabouts of the people who have been disappeared will be publicized immediately.
- To help in the rehabilitation of and extend cooperation to displaced people to return to their respective houses in a peaceful, comfortable and respectable manner.
- Return the properties of the leaders of political parties, activists and civilians, which were seized, locked up or prohibited from being used during the period of the conflict, to concerned persons or their families. Problems arising while returning the properties will be resolved through mutual agreement (GoN, 2006).

## Comprehensive Peace Accord (CPA )

CPN (Maoist) and the Government of Nepal signed the Comprehensive Peace Accord (CPA) on 21 November, 2006 (MOPR, 2011), made commitment to those children who had been involved in Nepal's decade armed conflict, (Partnerships for Protecting Children in Armed Conflict, 2010). CPA stipulated that those "children who have already been affected shall be rescued immediately and adequate provisions shall be made for their rehabilitation (CPA, 2006 p. 2).

The CPA makes a number of commitments especially to children. These include- i) an end to the misuse of schools, teachers and students for political purposes, ii) an end to discrimination based on age, sex, caste or ethnic origin, iii) an end to violence against children and child labor, and iv) an end to the use of children by armed groups (GoN, 2012, p. 22). Maintaining appropriate academic environment after the CPA has been ensured in the CPA. Also it has agreed on doing no any political activities in the school, harming teachers and students in any way, not using the students in the political programs in one or another way.

## According in Essence

Both sides agreed on respecting the rights of children, women and ensured on not doing any violence in and outside the school premises. Also the needed and appropriate assistance for the rehabilitation will be provided to the armed conflict affected children.

## National Plan of Action

The GoN has implemented the National Plan of Action (NPA) for Rehabilitation and Reintegration of Children Affected by Armed Conflict. The NPA aims to support the children affected by armed conflict and associated with the armed group. They are, i) minimizing vulnerability of re-recruitment, ii) reintegrating the children in the family and community, iii) mobilizing resources to develop functional collaboration and coordination with actors and stakeholders, and iv) formulating A comprehensive policy to address the issue strategically (NPA, 2012, p. 26). This plan aims to improve the reintegration process of the armed conflict affected in the society after the peace agreement.

## Three-Year Interim Plan (2007-2010)

The government's Three-Year Interim Plan 2007/08–2009/10 concerned the importance of protecting and promoting the fundamental rights of children, through the creation of a child-friendly environment encouraging for their overall development. Regarding ten years armed conflict affected children: it adopted strategies to expand and continue efforts to discharge and rehabilitate them, and increase their access to services and facilities. It prioritized armed conflict affected children in the eradication of all forms of mistreatment, discrimination, abuse, violence and hazards against children and aimed to bring them within the framework of social protection. It also emphasized the need to intensify programs focused on the effective rescue, rehabilitation and protection of CAAC, to establish Child Protection Centers at regional levels, to expand psychosocial counseling and rehabilitation services, and to ensure participation of children in the development of such programs.

## Three-Year Interim Plan (2010-2013)

The Three-Year Plan (2010/11-2012/13) has also the provision of helping the armed conflict affected children. It has also focused on the relief and rehabilitation, protection of conflict affected children. This three year interim plan of GoN has continued its support for (GoN, 2012, p. 28):

i. Implementing integrated and targeted programs for rehabilitation and reintegration (with the provisions of psychosocial counseling, education and skills) of the conflict affected children and children at risk (girl child, children with disability and of marginalized community, street children), and

ii. Establishing and operating 'Permanent Children's Fund' for the protection of the rights of the child as well as for providing emergency support and relief to the children who are at risk.

This plan has focused on the children's issues after CPA. For the implementation of the plan, GoN has provided a sum of NRs 10 million to the Children's Relief Funds and the Ministry of Women, Children and Social Welfare has developed a guideline for management of the fund so allowed.

## Ministry of Women, Children and Social Welfare

The Ministry of Women, Children and Social Welfare has implemented different program to support the conflict affected children. MWCSW implemented "short-term relief activities implemented under the Program on Protection and Management of Rural Children of Districts Highly Affected by the Conflict for children displaced by the conflict from districts in the Mid- and Far Western Development Regions and sheltered by the Nepal Children's Organizations in Kailali, Banke and Kapilvastu districts, including those reintegrated with their families. Similarly, socialization activities conducted through child clubs for CAAFAG following their discharge and return home" (MoPR & Mowcsw, 2010, p.

## 10 Year Plan for Children Welfare

The Ministry of Women, Children and Social Welfare has developed and started enactment of the 10-Year National Plan of Action for Children 2004–2014 to protect and promote the rights of children especially for the conflict affect children. Phases of plan this plan included programs to protect children from conflict and ensure the rights of conflict affected children. Similarly, another program, the Human Rights Action Plan 2007 includes various aspects of the rights of children, specifically addresses the protection and rehabilitation of children who are displaced, homeless and/or devoid of their family or anyone to take care of them as well as those in vulnerable situations (GoN, 2012).

## Ministry of Peace and Reconstruction

### *Welfare of Children Lost Their Parents*

Through the Ministry of Peace and Reconstruction, the government has delivered scholarships for the children of people killed during the conflict. "The Procedure for Financial Assistance, Relief and

Compensation to the Conflict Affected 2008 has stipulated that the State will provide free scholarships for a maximum of three children of those killed by the conflict, if their family is being provided with compensation by the government (MoPR, 2011). There is related providing for scholarships for up to three children of the disappeared According to action plan of Nepal government (2010) annual lump sum amounting to NRs 10,000 for primary, NRs 12,000 for lower secondary, NRs 14,000 for secondary and NRs 16,000 for certificate or higher secondary levels is provided to eligible children until the age of 18 years or Grade 12 (MoPR, 2010).

## Efforts of International Organizations and NGOs

With the affected children in the conflict era, different national and international organizations including UNICEF and Save the Children made discussions about the protection of child rights. These discussions led to form CZOP (Children as Zone of Peace) in 2003 for the protection of the children rights who are suffered in the armed conflict and in that era. The main aim of the CZOP is to combat the children from the effect of armed conflict.

## SZOPs Opened

Not only CZOP, SZOP (School as zone of Peace, of Zone) was also established for the protection of the children along with the school. The Annual General Assembly of the Coalition of the CZOP in 2008 has prioritized the issues of SZOP. It mainly focuses on children to have access to education into school without any disturbances by stopping, use of school premises and school children for political and arm related activities, school closure in blocked and transport or other strikes, and harassment to children in and outside of school etc. Moreover, it aims to encourage de-politicization and keeping the arm activities away from schools.

## Welfare Scheme for Students Vulnerable Situations

In 2006, international and national organizations working in the child protection sector, including UNICEF, Save the children and other organization lunched different program to strengthen the capacities of CAAFAG and to restore and enhance their roles in their families and their communities. The activities are lunched to provide CAAC, CAAFAG and other children in vulnerable situations with education, health services, livelihood opportunities, psychosocial counseling, awareness-raising, and reconciliation, prevention of re-recruitment into armed forces and groups, and community support (schools and community-based organizations).

## Country Specific Scenario on Conflict Affected Children

In this section, I have tried to present some specific conflict affected countries' practices to address the needs and demands of the conflict affected, particularly, the children in post conflict situations.

### Sierra Leone

The combatants, specially youths and children and the civilians are highly affected by the conflict in Sierra Leone. The youths are highly traumatized by the war and they are deprived of their civil rights, social and economic existence in the society. After the conflict, many programs are held for the reintegration. The successful social and economic reintegration of the youths who are engaged in the conflict directly and indirectly has been one of the good examples for the resolution of the conflict.

### An Approach of Development Organisations

The Government of Sierra Leone, different development organizations has used, "the specific crisis-sensitive approach to target to conflict affected children, focused on local capacities and community orientation, mainstreamed reconciliation and peace building activities in skills training and involved different stakeholders at both local and national level" (Mai, 2011, p. 3). By this program, most of the children were engaged to develop their technical skills. The government provided them the school fees and other help for education.

## Capacity Development Approach: Highlighted

They focused on capacity development approach, strengthening their capacities through vocational training. By this training, the children were able to put their marketable skills to sustained economic use. Community based approach has been very relevant for the conflict affected and child soldiers after conflict in the case of Sierra Leone. Basically, the skill based training has helped the children and youths in the society which has helped them to tie their relationship with the member of the society and it has finally led to build up the financial and social situation.

## Tajikistan

The Government of Tajikistan and the International Organization for Migration (IOM) the project's executing agency, in cooperation with local authorities organized a long term program (income-generation alternative program) to sustain the livelihood of the conflict affected children in Tajikistan (UNDP, 2010). After the training, 95% participants were making sustainable livelihood. There was stumpy education relief package and technical package was mostly effective there.

## Colombia

Re-integration Policy. After the ceasefire in Colombia, the Office of the High Counselor for the reintegration (ACR) has been in charge of the reintegration policy. The ACR assisted the conflict affected children by providing education, vocational training, and grants for micro business projects, psychological support, and health care. According to Saenz (2012), the children received more /less financial support depending on their participation in education and vocational training. There was provision of higher job opportunity for those who had the greater education level. So there was more interest of children in education rather than in other assistance. And the government was also seen more sensitive to what the conflict affected wanted.

## Liberia

### *An Indispensable Relief Program*

In Liberia, due to the economic crisis, the government was not able to provide indispensable relief program to their conflict affected children. By the help of NGO and civil societies, it is said that, "the children were receiving little amount of money per month from DDR reinsertion package" (Forsther, 2011, p. 12). The conflict affected children of Liberia had low interest in formal educational level, but very high interest in vocational training skill and other technical education. However, the high rate of vocational training skills amongst the children did not necessarily reflect their employment (Paes, 2005). The vocational training provided to the conflict affected children has not led them to find the employment. "The new skills also didn't help them, the children of the conflict affected were unfortunately the highest unemployed groups of people in Monrovia" (Forsther, 2011, p. 50). It seems that the skill provided to them for the livelihood also doesn't matter in some cases for the conflict affected.

## Basic Reasons of Unemployment Situations

And they are finding it difficult to cope with the life during the post-conflict reconstruction due to their less qualification and untrustworthiness, which led to high unemployment amongst them. Moreover, they become vulnerable to politician and other potential spoilers because of their lack of proper education in making sound decisions.

## Mozambique

### *Subsidy in Education Grained*

In Mozambique, the government and the civil society were seen more responsible to socialize the war affected children. The government granted subsidy in education and other vocational trainings and encouraged the war affected .children to be there (Ozerdem & Podder, 2011). And children have been assisted in education by the government and they saw their career in education and continued their education. Most of the war affected children became trusted and productive adult members of their communities and nation by means of education. And they were able to participate in income generating activities.

## Post Conflict Situation and Children Reintegration

### *Intering Relief Program*

The Twelve-Point Agreement signed by the Seven-Party Alliance (SPA) and the CPN (Maoist), on 22 November, 2005 along with the successive popular peaceful movement of April, 2006 brought an end to the armed conflict in Nepal (Nepal Institute for Policy Studies, 2013). This study reasserted that the Nepali government created a multi-agency task force to gather data of conflict affected and provide them assistances. According to GoN (2012), it is stated that in 2008, Nepal created the Interim Relief Program (IRP) in an attempt to address the identified immediate needs of those harmed children and other people by the former government or the Maoists. Although the delays, confusions and contradictions among the major stakeholders on integration and rehabilitation, ultimately, "the major political parties took a historic decision on 1 November, 2012 and signed a Seven-Point Agreement on integration and rehabilitation of the former combatants and other armed conflict affected children" (NIPS, 2013, p. 9).

## Criterion of Relief Packages

### *Interim Relief Program*

1. NPR 100,000 Nepalese rupees (approximately US $1,400 in 2008) to the nearest beneficiary of those who were killed, or who were forcibly disappeared by parties to the conflict.
2. NPR 25,000 each to the widows of men who died or the wives of those who were forcibly disappeared during the conflict (in addition to the NPR 100,000 above).
3. "Scholarships" for children of persons killed, forcibly disappeared, or seriously disabled during the conflict.
4. Reimbursement of medical expenses or treatment at a government hospital for a specified level of disability or injury resulting from the conflict.
5. Skills development training for eligible conflict affected.
6. Compensation for persons and institutions whose real or personal property was lost or damaged during the conflict.

(NIPS, 2013)

According to the CPA ,"there will be relief packages available to those whose near ones were killed and disappeared, or who were maimed, displaced, and affected and those whose properties were damaged in the armed conflict" (NIPS, 2013, p. 19).

Special facilities under Interim constitution, 2007.Similarly, Interim Constitution (2007) stated that "the helpless, orphan, mentally retarded, conflict affected, displaced, vulnerable and street children shall have the right to get special facilities from the state for their well-ascertained future" (p. 3). In 2008, Nepal created the Interim Relief Program (IRP) in an attempt to address the identified immediate needs of those harmed children and other people by the former government or the CPN (Maoist). However, the IRP has not adequately met the immediate or long term needs or expectations expressed by the conflict affected children and other people (IHRC, 2013).

## Extent of Success

This study furthermore highlighted that "the IRP, scheduled to end in 2014, however, has not fully met affected needs and expectations, and the commission as proposed would fall short as well" (p. 1). It is true because of massive impacts on armed conflict like physical, psychological, and socioeconomic well-being of affected. So it required different types of provision and support to deal with these effects of affected. "Some need financial aid to meet their basic needs. Looking to the future, they spoke about the importance of job training, employment opportunities, educational support for their children, and assistance with medical expenses for both physical and mental harm" (IHRC, 2013, p. 3). Therefore the provided programs are provided without the need analysis of conflict affected. Owing to this, these are so it was inadequate and not sufficient as per the need of conflict affected. Also the trainings on vocational education was targeted to provide in all 75 districts but was only existed in 12 districts but the affected interest was in another sides as their interest is not heard (IHRC, 2013).

## Programs: Proved Insufficient Deal with

Thus, provided limited relief programs were not sufficient to fulfill basic need and ensure conflict affected children future life. And neither they have get adequate support from the family for their reintegration because of the extreme poverty nor from the government for sustainable livelihood. Because, IRP has not mentioned exactly to provide education and related relief programs as per the desire of conflict affected children .It made these children more frustration and hindrance in post conflict situation. So the traumatized and self-stigmatized children's condition is being more miserable.

## Children are Still Neglected

Thus, it can to be said that the children are still suffering from the consequences of the armed conflict. They seem like orphans, helpless, and searching the helping hand to get socialized and to survive in their society. The armed conflict affected children felt that they have low and poor academic achievement and felt themselves backward in education so they do not want to continue their study. In their voices, they should have other alternatives for secured livelihood.

## Research Related to My Study

### *A Group of Pre*

It is necessary to find out what has already been explored in the related field before starting a research venture. So, I went through some related research works carried out in this field which I have discussed briefly along the following paragraphs.

### *Treatise Scripted Written*

While searching the literatures regarding the children involvement in the conflict and its effect, I found Machel's (1996) study on the impact of armed conflict on children, which is taken as the first and the most renowned comprehensive human rights assessment on the conflict affected children. This study has explored the plight of internally displaced children, child soldiers, child affected of sexual violence and landmines, and the psychological impact of war on children between 1986 A.D. to 1996 A.D. The study concluded that the children who were being affected by war had suffered from deep emotional stress and thus needed psychological counseling.

### *Perusal of Study by Counsels*

Wessells (1998) also focused on the stress that the children were facing after the armed conflict affected children. The study revealed that the conflict had caused depression, changed attitudes and diminished hopes for the future. The study concluded that the children in the post conflict situation were facing several challenges and problems. Similarly, Brett, McCallin, and O'Shea (1996) in a book "Children: The Invisible Soldiers" have focused poverty, disruption of social environment, desire of revenge and power as the main reasons for why the children were participating in wars. In this context, the children were motivated to become part of the armed conflict and their educational achievement had been ended by the war.

### *Work of Two Research Fellows*

In two distinct studies on armed conflict in Sri Lanka, Somasundaram (2002) and Hogg (2006) concluded that social, cultural and political issues were the main factors for the participation of the children in conflicts. Also these studies focused that the violence against

Tamils, government unaccountability, disruption of education, food insecurity, and displacement had pushed the children to participate in the armed conflict. This situation was similar with the children from the Dalit, marginalized and socially excluded community in Nepal who faced different kinds of discrimination and as a result participated in the armed conflict.

### *Study of Similar Event in Other Companies*

Pradhan's study (2012) on "Sri Lanka's Armed Conflict: Children as Affected and Agents of Peace" focused on children used in armed conflict and its effect on their life in post conflict situation. According to Pradhan, Sri Lanka had faced almost three decades long civil war which affected the lives of millions of civilians. He furthermore reasserted that the six grave violations against children during armed conflicts included killing or maiming of children, recruitment or use of child soldiers, rape and sexual violence, abduction of children, attacks against schools and hospitals and denial of humanitarian access to children. Based on this study, it can be said that children were highly affected by the three decade long armed conflict in Sri Lanka. This study highlighted the importance of children's involvement in peace building efforts such as the reconciliation, recovery, and Disarmament, Demobilization and Reintegration (DDR) processes, in order to achieve long-term stability and durable peace.

### *Study of Conflict of Gnaristion*

In a study on armed conflict and children's experiences and situation in Afghanistan, Aittokoski (2013) focuses on the hardships of the conflict affected children in the post conflict situation. The affected did not have adequate resources to cope with the situation. Aittokoski also talkes about the support provided to the affected in the post conflict situation which was not sufficient. In addition, the material and emotive necessity were not being satisfied. Also the community around them was not supporting the affected and acceptance had been a problem which resulted in post-traumatic situation where the physical, emotional, social and spiritual wellbeing were the major risks for the affected children.

### *Case – Study on Conflict in South Kivn*

Sbovodova (2012) conducted a case study on the impact of armed conflict on sexual violence against minor in South Kivu, Democratic Republic of Congo. Sbovodova highlighted the sexual violence of the women, girls and children during the armed conflict. There were several cases of the rape and sexual harassment to the family members which resulted in the post-traumatic stress disorder on the affected children, girls and women. In this study, the military officials were found to be involved in the rape cases.

### *Arino's Study of Nepal*

Arino (2008) has also conducted a study entitled "Nepal: Gender view of the armed conflict and the peace agreement". This study has highlighted how women suffer the sexual violence and how they perceive it. Both the state security forces and the CPN (Maoist) exploited women sexually, ignoring the strict codes of conduct in the armed group in order to prevent misbehavior, including that of a sexual nature. The state security force has mainly targeted the women combatants and their family for the sexual violence. So they were facing real challenges in the rehabilitation in the society after the peace agreement.

Similarl.y, in a report of ICRC (2011) on children affected by the armed conflict and other situations of violence has focused on the acceptance of the armed conflict children in the society and family.

Mutual acceptance is the major weapon for the reintegration of the affected in the society and community. The children are still not accepted in the society because of the fear of being rejected. So the impact of conflict has resulted in high risks of the adverse reactions.

## Study by Gautam 2007

The study conducted by Gautam (2007) on the impact of armed conflict on children focused on the impact of the conflict in various ways like, sexual violence, maiming, abduction, disappearance. The study showes that those acts were done by both the state security forces and the CPN (Maoist). The school going children were tortured. The security forces had charged the children being involved in CPN (Maoist) activities. The cases of re-arrest of the children had significantly led the psychological problems to the children. They are blamed by both the parties of spying against them. So the school going children were facing several effects then, and similar emotional and psychological effects in the post conflict situation as well.

## Theoretical Underpinnings

### *Definitions of the Term "Resilience"*

Resilience is best defined as "the ability of a system to absorb disturbances and still retain its basic function and structure" (Walker & Salt, 2006, p. 1). Another scholar defined that resilience is the capacity to change in order to maintain the same identity (Folke et al., 2010). In addition, the concept of resilience in relation to social–ecological systems incorporates the idea of adaptation, learning and self-organization in addition to the general ability to persist disturbance (Folke, 2006). So resilience means return of human being to return in the previous condition after some causalities like natural disaster, conflicts etc.

### *Several Definitions of Resilience*

Different scholars defined resilience in various ways. Rutter (1987, 1990), for example, has characterized resilience as the constructive end of the allocation of developmental outcomes among individuals at high risk. So, resilience can be understood as the development of positive thinking capacity after the involvement of the people in the severe hazards. Resilience can be defined as the ability of an energetic system to endure or recover from significant challenges that threaten its stability, viability, or development (Masten 2011, 2012). In short, resilience is a concept which has two dimensions, the first one is to get the exposure on the different hazards, risks and the second one is to get the successful overcome of those risks and becomes competent to live an individual life. Hence, resilience is the ability to 'bounce back' after experiencing a particularly difficult or challenging situation. It is not something that some people have and others do not. But it is like a process that helps people get through traumatic experiences of natural disaster and armed conflict etc. and cope with stress and adversity. It is a process determined by a person's inner strengths and external support structures.

Liebenberg and Ungar (2011) have also highlighted resilience theory as the understanding that humans have "the ability to overcome adverse conditions and to function normally in the face of risk," is of particular relevance to the environment that they live. This shows that the ability to trounce the human threats in the abnormal condition is resilience theory.

Studies (for example, Boothby et al., 2006; Blattman, 2010) show that when former child soldiers who were affected by the conflict and have direct involvement in the armed conflict in Mozambique and Uganda, they were provided with rehabilitative and psychosocial supports and embraced by their communities, finally they became productive adults who are needed for the development of the nation.

Similarly, in another study done by International Youth Foundation (2011) also suggests that deeply traumatized youth can turn into productive citizens. The resilience of youth should therefore, be directed and nurtured, with youth individual seen as a resource and partner in the overall development.

## Resilience Theory: As Theory for Affected People

Here, resilience theory is seen as the practice and the therapy for the affected people by various reasons like conflict, natural disasters, etc. It is much more relevant in terms of conflict affected children who are overcoming the adverse situation in the present situation by developing themselves as the potential and active member of the society for the development of the nation. In this study also, it seems the same case. The study is about the educational adversities of the conflict affected children and how they are overcoming the pains by their present survival and adjustment in the society in a normal life. So, exactly the resilience theory meets the pre determinants of the nature that the study is conducted within the conflict affected children and their present survival. So my study is guided by the principles of resilience.

## Capability Approach

I have also examined from the research concern from the capability approach. Sen (1993) stats that capability approach is both a social evaluation tool and a policy design, which focuses on what people are able to do and be, on the quality of their life, and on removing hindrances in their lives so that they have more liberty to living the compassionate of life which, upon reflection, they find valuable. Thus, it is a tool which focuses that people are effectively able to do and to be, that is, on their capabilities. This approach concentrates on people's happiness and practical approaches that concentrate on income, expenditures, consumption or basic needs fulfillment (Sen, 1993).

## Role of Capability Approach

According to Sen, capability approach also helps to identify the social constrictions that influence and confine both well-being as well as the evaluative exercises. The capability approach can also be used to measure shortage or inequality, or can be used as an alternative for traditional utilitarian cost-benefit analysis.

## Capability: As Freedom to Achieve and to do Valuable Thing

Similarly, Sen's Capabilities Approach (1993) affirmed that capability is the freedom to achieve valuable beings and doings. Sen focused on the freedom of choices for the development of individuals. The main theme of the capability approach is the distinction between the means and the ends of well-being and development. It also holds that only the ends have intrinsic importance, whereas means are only instrumental to reach the goal of increased well-being and development. Sen (1995) stressed on the role of agency, the process of choice and the freedom to reason in the selection of relevant capabilities.

## Combination of Functioning

Sen (1997) also focused on the freedom of choices with alternative combinations of functioning for their life contributing to reducing poverty, enhancing the capability and balancing the power structure.

## Analysis of Capability Deprivation

Sen (1999) considered poverty as sensibly identified in terms of capability deprivation. In this regards, he suggests that poverty situation can be improved by focusing not only on generating economic growth but by enhancing people's intrinsically important capabilities. Sen reasserts that the major advantage of 'freedoms' is that they put much more emphasis on the choices of the person in need rather than the interests and policies of the aid giver. So the availability of education is a primary freedom for a child and the method of education may enhance those freedoms based on the education of the conflict affected children. With the capability approach, it can be said that only after fulfilling the demands with the need analysis and freedom of choices, the life of the people would be sustainable and peace agreement will have a successful ending.

## Points in Focus of Capability Approach

The capability approach focuses on what conflict affected are able to do and be, as opposed to what they have, or how they feel in present. The capability approach does contribute a new and useful perspective on conflict affected children by differentiating two levels of the problem: the capability level and the functioning level. That means it is also useful for understanding the causes of being affected. Similarly, this approach allows researchers to analyze how these conflict affected were in the conflict period. It also guides to find the obstacles and risks of those conflicts affected to reintegrate in their society in the post conflict situations.

## Focus on Providing Freedom

This approach focuses on providing the freedom to these affected to choose their interested skill base education, training to develop their career for their future life. It means that what conflict affected are effectively able to do and to be; that is, on their capabilities. So I argue this approach properly fit into my research.

## Gap-I Noticed

AN EVALUATION: The studies which were related to the armed conflict helped me to find the gap of my study. The empirical research shows overall concept of the situation of the armed conflict from different perspectives. The studies were mainly focused on the children's involvement in the armed conflict, the violence that they faced, challenges after the post conflict for the social reintegration; the post traumatic situations and the support they get were discussed. Shakya (2006) has only focused on how the children were becoming affected of armed conflict but she is lacking consequences of armed conflict on children education, and conflict affected children social acceptances after the peace agreement. Similarly, Gatuam (2007) studied about the internal conflict, its impact on children, international commitment to protect the right of children and implementation of state commitment and obligation during to period of armed conflict in Nepal. This study focused on all the conflict affected children but I have limited my study within the school children affected experiencing, their education during the period of conflict and coping strategy after the peace agreement which is lacking in previous study.

So, this study on the experiences of the school going children during the conflict and their adversities in the post conflict situation has tried to fulfill the gap. My aim, therefore, is to fulfill the gap between the impacts of the conflict on children and their adversities to reintegrate them in the society.

## How Does this Study Unique?

Since the analysis of the conflict affected was not analyzed in other studies, this study differs from the previous research works to the extent that it is more comprehensive evidences on the educational experiences of the school children during the conflict and the adversities after the post conflict situation. Thus, in brief it is introspection, review analysis of present works or pruning and decorticating or fleecing them that has bestowed this work unique identity – I can proclaim this now with

## Summary of the Chapter

This chapter dealt with the review of various published literatures. I reviewed the literature concerned with the main areas of interest in this study. Through these literatures, I discussed international and national children convention and protocols which are concerned with the protection of children in armed conflict situations and discussed the ideas of different writers about armed conflict and its effect on livelihood. Then, I presented the theory guiding my study. Finally, the chapter ended with the gaps between the existing policies, practices, experiences and present situation of the conflict affected.

# 3

# Research Methods

This chapter gives a detailed description of the methodology that has been used in this study. Mainly, this chapter is presented in two parts. The first part deals with the philosophical approaches, and the second part deals with the procedural approaches. Within the philosophical approaches, I have introduced the research paradigm, epistemological and ontological stances, and methodological issues. On the other hand, in the procedural approach I have discussed, the study of location and site, tools of data collection, selection of the research participants, etc. Finally, I have presented the trustworthiness and ethical considerations of the study at the end of this chapter.

## Qualitative Research: An Approach of my Enquiry

Qualitative research focuses on interpretation of phenomena in its natural setting, to make sense in terms of the meanings people bring to the setting (Creswell, 2007). This research also aims to make the meanings of the real affected in their natural settings. The purpose of this study is to explore the school children's experiences of education and their present situation after the peace agreement.

## An Interpretive Enquiry

Qualitative research is a form of interpretive inquiry in which the researchers make interpretation of what they hear, see and understand as such interpretations are not separable from their own history, background and context (Creswell, 2011, p. 175). I wanted to explore experiences of the school going children during the armed conflict through these methods which attempt to get an in-depth opinion from participants (Dawson, 2002). So, I have collected the experiences, their feelings and their daily experiences through interviewing as "knowledge is constituted in large part by the manner in which it is communicated (e.g., speech, writing, dance, gestures, silence) and that alternative forms of knowledge require appropriate modes of representation" (Taylor & Wallace, 2007, p. 3). I have also enquired about the experiences of the participants based on the methodology that I have used to explore the social problem, experiences (Creswell, 2012) to comprehend the participants' realities.

## Patterns and Purpose of Participants Behavior

It is well conceived that qualitative method is the best approach to study the phenomenon of the participants as it enables researchers to see the patterns and purpose of each participant's behavior and perspectives. Denzin and Lincoln (2003) stated that "qualitative research is a field of inquiry in its own right which is a complex, interconnected family of terms, concepts and assumptions" (p. 3). In this view I designed this study to explore the complexities and realities of the school going children during and after the ten years armed conflict. In my study, qualitative case study method is applied as it aims to collect their life experiences (Hartley, 2004). In doing so, I have adapted Flick's (2006) essential features of qualitative research in which I have looked for appropriateness of methods and theories, incorporated perspectives of the participants and their diversity along with reflectivity of the researcher and the research. Many daily communications with conflict affected, rely on such shared experiences (Cohen, Manion, & Morrison, 2007) of the conflict affected in my study.

## Paradigmatic Consideration: Interpretive Stand

A philosophical consideration, as a tool, provides us with the essential principles about the world, encourages and delves us in a deeper understanding of the nature of the inquiry itself. "It is a comprehensive belief system which guides research and practice in a field; any researcher needs to have a certain paradigm to view the research area" (Willis, 2007, p. 8). Philosophical approach provides idea to the researcher to maintain his or her position in the research study. It is very useful in any kind of research to determine the appropriate methodology and design tools. While talking about the philosophical consideration, different researchers have different points of view to get the date for the research.

My study is guided by the interpretive stand of the qualitative research. It is much more reflected by the phenomenological case study method through the in-depth interview with the participants. In my study, I aim to generate reflective understanding of the participants in context. It is characterized by a concern for the individual whose central endeavor is to understand the subjective world of human experiences. So the participant's experiences have been explored by using phenomenological case studies (Luitel, *Settlemaier*, & Taylor, 2011). Basically, I interpret what the participants shared about their experiences. As a result, multiple realities are constructed where subjective reality play a crucial role in shaping and affecting the realities of the participants. So as a passionate participant, I inquired the voices of the conflict affected facilitating the "multi-voice" (Denzin & Lincoln, 1994) reconstruction.

## Technical Standard: Complied with

No matter how close, I come to meet the detailed technical standards for a research; the result of my study is not an objective report of the reality of the matter (Willis, 2007). I have tried to include myself with the participants and the area of my research has very close relationship to explore the experiences in an interesting way (Walsham, 2005). In this respect, I have stressed on the analysis of the contexts (Reeves & Hedberg, 2003) during the interview with the subjective meanings that lie behind the social phenomenon of the participants (Kaplan & Maxwell, 1994).

## Subjective Meanings of Experiences

"The core idea of interpretivism in my study is to work with the subjective meanings of the experiences of participants, i.e. to acknowledge their existence, to understand them, to use them as building blocks in theorizing" (Goldkuhl, 2012). So being a researcher of the interpretive paradigm, my stance in the study is aimed at understanding the experiences of the school going children during and after the peace agreement. In the process, multiple meanings are generated and the meanings from the subjective interpretivism have guided me towards the goal by making the interpreted meaning sensible.

## Phenomenological Case Study: My Methodology

I have adopted a qualitative phenomenological case study approach in this study. Tesch (1994, as cited in Gray, 2014) has also highlighted: *"phenomenological research is more focused on the human experience of the life-world"* (p. 24). I wanted to explore the school children's' experiences of education during the ten years armed conflict. I adopted this method because, "it involves the use of thick description and close analysis of lived experience to understand how meaning is created through embodied perception" (Sokolowski, 2000). It helps to understand the deeper understanding of the lived experiences of the participants. In my study, the phenomenon is education of conflict affected children and their educational experience is the phenomenology.

## Previous Experience is Pygmy,. Yet Important

I have little knowledge about the ten years armed conflict effect on children's education as I had experienced in my school age. When recalling my school age, I remember the news about the CPN (Maoist) attacks, death of many people, injuries and disappearance. I was unable to analyze the case at that time. It is noteworthy to recall one of my experiences here. My father was a teacher in a primary school. As per the CPN (Maoist) requests, he gave some amount of money as a *levy* (cash donation) and sometimes, gave shelter and foods. As a result, the state security force arrested my father three times, blamed him to be a CPN (Maoist) supporter and put him into the Jail for some months. After the arrest of my father, the state security force regularly came to my house and tortured my mother and me. In such a circumstance, I was unable to concentrate on my studies. This led me to be a weak student who had, relegated from the first boy of the class. I used to recall it sometimes and wanted to compare the educational attainment of the students who have the same situation during the armed conflict. So, the little knowledge has also led me to use phenomenology which Sokolowski (2000) quotes as, the clear and essential aspects, that are previously known and not the new one though they are still vital and informative and makes the researchers confused in the importance and clearness of the study in phenomenological case studies.

## Impact of an Acquatiance

Likewise, there are so many school children who faced homologous situation what I faced during my school years. So, I was more interested in developing a more in depth study about how the school children experienced their education during the armed conflict and about the coping adversities in the post conflict situation after peace agreement. To explore the experiences of school children and coping adversities I used phenomenological case study in my study. A phenomenological study, which is designed to describe experiences and the contexts of those experiences, is the qualitative approach I chose to use for this study of the school going children experiences of ten years armed conflict because it is the qualitative method best suited to my research question: a phenomenological study describes the meaning for school children's lived experiences of a concept or a phenomenon (Creswell, 2007).

## Interviews or Specific Type Conduced

I have tried to focus on the close examination of the participant's individually to capture the meaning and phenomenological common features, or essences, of an experience of the conflict as Starks and Trinidad (2007) said. Phenomenological case study helps to explore the reality based on the embodied experiences. Creswell (2013) states that phenomenological case study explores a multiple bound systems (cases) over time, throughout detailed, in-depth data collection involving various sources of information (like observations, interviews, audio visual objects, and documents and reports) and reports of a case narrative and case-based themes. (p. 7)

## Phenomenological Case Study

Therefore, I found that phenomenological case study was suitable for my research to get into the depth of it and to gain insight into how the school going children experienced education particularly during the ten years armed conflict and what kind of adversities they are facing in the post conflict in Gorkha district. Thus, I have considered it as more suitable to the heterogeneity and difficulty on my research topic and site. I think case study best suits my research issues as I am going to collect, analyze and represent the school going children's experiences of education during the armed conflict.

## Case – Study: Exploration of Perception

Yin (2014) suggests the case study as a particular style of educational research which may be appropriate for exploring the participants' perception of a particular movement. So the phenomenological case studies have been employed to explore the lived experiences of the participants which mean an intensive description and the analysis of a single or of groups (Yin, 2003). He restates that case studies tackle on those subject matters about which the researcher has some or little knowledge previously known or fundamentally flawed. Arguing with Yin, I have used phenomenological case study in this study. I have explored multiple experiences of the school going children through interview, observation and focus group discussion with their family (Kershner & Chaplin, 2001). I dug out rich and thick multiple realities of the participants (Flick, 2009) through the phenomenological case study on school children experience in armed conflict.

## Experiences or Children During and After Armed Conflict

As my research focuses on the experiences of school children during the armed conflict and their present adversities in reintegrating in the society, it focuses on the descriptions of experience as it actually appeared in the participants' consciousness. So, I was not to test hypothesis but to get individuals to reflect thoughtfully about what they would see, feel and believe regarding the overall concept of teaching reading and making the students motivated towards extensive reading.

## Epistemology and Ontology: Subjective, Context Oriented and Multiple

Geven (2008) defines ontology as the study of existence: the most general branch of metaphysics concerned with the nature of being.

Hence, what is reality or truth is determined by the position of the researcher's ontology as Willis (2007) says that ontology is concerned with the nature of reality and various ontological positions, reflect different prescriptions of what can be the real and what cannot be. Opie (2004) also views that ontological assumption as it helps to determine the persons social reality and the characteristic of the social world as external, autonomous, given and objectively real or instead, as a socially built and subjectively proficient.

## Scope of Study on Time-Scale

As far as my study is concerned, ontologically, the study and its findings are subjective (Van Maanen, 1990) with conflict affected experiences within the ten years' armed conflict during the period 1996 to 2006 and after the peace agreement. Since my participants were affected differently, they experienced their school education differently in their contexts, they interpreted the reality of their experience and coping adversities accordingly based upon their context and experience. That's why, I got varieties of responses to my questions and differences in their experiences while observing their lessons because knowledge is personal, subjective and unique (Cohen et al., 2000, p. 6). In my case, the reality of their experiences in ten years armed conflict and coping adversities in the post conflict situation is not confined within a single strategy; instead, it was wide-ranging from person to person, context to context and situation to situation in spite of having similarities in most cases.

## Epistemological Stand: Defined

Regarding my epistemological stance, I strongly support the idea of Richards (2003) that the exploration of the social interaction of the individual with the environment in which people live and work enables us to understand the ways in which the world is interpreted and common understandings are created. Hence, human beings construct meanings as they engage with the world they are interpreting. So was the case in my study because there was different accident that experimented by school going children during the period of ten years conflict and aftermath the peace agreement. The school children explored their experienced according to the situation and context and they interpreted the reality based on such experience. In this way; I emphasized the accounts given by my participants based on their experiences. I got various experiences and adversities during the period of the armed conflict and after the peace agreement. I believe these differences were the outcomes of their lived experience which I found different from one individual to another (Cohen et al., 2000).

## Participants Difference Experiences: Worth Collection

So the single reality of a single participant did not play vital role to explore the effect of the ten years long armed conflict on their education during that period and on education and livelihood in the post conflict situation. For this, I dug out the participants' different experiences towards my particular issue. For which, an analysis of multiple realities was required (Creswell, 2012). Based on this ground, I was guided by the participants various experiences (Flick, 2009). Thus, I believe that knowledge is relative and it depends on each participant's varied experiences. Hence this study is guided by the subject reality.

## Research Site, Participants and Data

This research is carried in Gorkha district one or the highly conflict affected district during the period of armed conflict (United Nations Office of the High Commissioner for Human Rights, 2012) and carried among four participants of the district as the small size is useful for analyzing the data properly in a qualitative research (Creswell, 2003, p. 18). Although the total sample size is relatively small, the selected number permits me to generate sufficient variety and depth of data. Onwuegbuize and Leech (2007) also focus on the importance of using small size sample in the qualitative research. They focus on, "Sample sizes in qualitative research, should not be so large that it become difficult to extract thick, rich data" (p. 242).

## Scope of Study from Various Angles

The scope of the study is to explore the present situation of ten years armed conflict affected children and their academic life and this study is limited to those children who were under the age of eighteen in the era of ten years armed conflict (1996-2006). Particularly those school children are the participants who were directly affected by the ten year armed conflict due to the fact that their family members were engaged in it, or were killed by either side (the state security force and the CPN-M of that period). Therefore, the participants of this study confine to those conflict affected children.

## Purposive Sampling for Cases

The three participants are selected on the basis of purposive sampling, which focuses more on criterion purposive sampling that involves searching for cases or individuals who meet a certain criterion (Cohen et al., 2000) and one participant is selected through snowball sampling.

## Selection of a Suitable Name or Site and Works

In the research site (i.e. in Gorkha), I could visit all research participants easily so that relevant data could be captured more effectively because it is better to choose that place where anyone can enter easily or it should be the place where it is possible for any to enter (Maxwell, 1996). Finally, I found some research works on conflict affected peoples' experiences internationally and nationally but no research work related to my topic has, as yet, been carried out in Nepal. Thus, this would be some kind of contribution to the field on reintegration of conflict affected children in post conflict society.

## Methodology for Collection or Data

There were different sources of data. Basically in my research study, the data's were collected from field notes, memos, and recordings of the interview as the primary data sources. According to Nunan (1993), "Secondary research consists of reviewing the literature in a given area, synthesizing the research carried out by others" (p. 8). All the materials available in print and electronic media, which are related to the proposed study, are consulted as the secondary source of data. For the secondary source, the journal articles, books, previous thesis, reports etc. which are in the print or the electronic media are used.

## Tools and Technique of Data Collection (In – Depth Interview)

In each and every research, there are some specific tools to be used according to the need and subject matter of the study. The process of data collection is an act performed by the educational researcher that provides a deeper understanding and exploration of the lived experiences and reality from the research participants (Strauss & Corbin, 1998, as cited in Dangal, 2010, p. 67). Thus, being a phenomenological case study researcher, I have used in- depth interview as a tool to collect data in this study.

## Interview: With Key Informants

I conducted the interview with the affected children during the ten years armed conflict and I considered such participants as "key informants" (Patton, 1990). I have used in depth interview with the participant to obtain the information in line with my research questions (Cohen et al., 2007). And other scholars have also identified different forms of interview like structured interview, semi-structured and unstructured types, I used semi-structured format; though some emergent questions were also generated and asked, which were of more flexible type and allowed for a depth of feeling to be ascertained by probing and eliciting insightful responses.

## A Search for Conflict Affected Individuals

At first, I called three participants over the phone after getting their contact numbers and visited all the participants personally in their working places and also at their homes. After calling the first participant Sarada of my study, I asked her if there were other conflict affected like her and she recommended Khim. She remembered Khim as one of the conflict affected who was also a member of the PLA. She briefed some information about Khim. I thought, he would be another participant of my study so I called him after getting his number from Sarada. After this, I informed them about the purpose of my research study in order to build rapport with them and requested them to participate in this research study. After this, I asked them to set the time for interview according to their convenience and planned schedule for interview on the basis of participants' wish. And I told them that I certainly would not disclose their name and view publicly without their consent. I assured my participants that I would highly maintain the confidentiality. Most of the questions were open-ended throughout the interview in order to encourage participants to respond freely and openly.

During the interview, I tried to explore the experiences of the participant based on the research questions. Then, I guided them to recall my research questions. It was more of an informal type, I simply listened to what my respondents were saying and sometimes asked them to explain how they felt about the situation they were describing as suggested (Richards, 2003).

## Visit at Side or Place of Participants

I went to the field after I finished preparing tools and provoking themes by consulting with my supervisor. The participants of my study were interviewed between February 15 and May 17, 2015 for the initial phase of the interview. I went directly to the place of the participant for their convenience as in their given time. I stayed in my study place continuously for a week near the participants' home and sometimes stayed in their rooms too.

## Interview: Face to Face

I conducted all of the interviews face to face which lasted up to two hour in average. I met the participants for more than three times in their convenient time. To record the data with care, I used a notebook with the knowledge and permission of the respondents and took some picture and short video as the problem of load shading. However, particular consideration was given to confidentiality, ethics and rights of the interviewees.

## Data Transcription Conducted

I started to transcribe the data collected when I took the in–depth interview. I was so careful when I was transcribing the data. When I felt confused then I looked at the video and read the note book. Also I called them when I felt that the enough data was not gathered and something was missing when I started writing their cases. After transcribing the data, again I held a round of interview the following day, and I presented the transcripts among the participants to ensure their accuracy.

## Data Analysis and Interpretation: Organisation of Information

Data analysis and interpretation is the main part of any research works. It is also known as the core heart of the entire research. But I felt that it is a very difficult task to analyze the data. It is also highlighted as, "data analysis is not a simple description of the data collected but a process by which the researcher can bring interpretation to the data" (Powney & Watt, 1987, as cited in Sook, 2003, p. 13). He further quotes Wiersma (1995) as, "Qualitative data analysis requires organization of information and data reduction. Thus, the researcher is required to organize and select related information from disordered, unorganized and discursive data" (as cited in Sook, 2003, p. 13).

## An Analysis Conducted

Aftermath, data and interpretation are interlinked with each other. After all, analysis in qualitative research is a process of successive approximation towards an accurate description and interpretation of the phenomena (Wiersma, 1995, as cited in Sook, 2003, p. 13).

Creswell (2003) mentions six steps of data analysis. In the first phase of data analysis, I made data ready for analysis and explanation in relation to the participants' understanding and meaning making on the children's experiences of education during the conflict. Then, I went through all the transcribed interviews again and again that I had written. After this, I arranged and sorted it into different categories on the basis of the obtained information.

## A General Sense of Participant Perspectives

In the second phase, I went through all the data thoroughly and attempted to make a general sense of participant's perspectives and constructed the meanings as a whole. In this phase, the meanings are made based on the interviews that are transcribed. Then, thirdly, I started analyzing in detail by giving codes to the participants and used the coding by using pseudonym Sarada, Mahadev, Khim and Radhika. This helped me to access the information easily. In the fourth phase, I began analyzing the themes using the same coding process that was implied in the third phase.

### Theme Generation & Description

After that I generated the themes and described all on the basis of interview. Furthermore, I described what happened in the interview in a narrative, only then described, discussed and interpreted them. In this aspect, I have written cases of the participants in the narrative form which supports the first research questions. And I have generated themes to support the responses for the second research question. After this, I compared the practices and understandings of the data to find out similarities and dissimilarities.

### Interpretation & Conclusion Phase of Work

Finally, at the last stage, I interpreted the data and drew the conclusion at the end of each theme along with the findings and discussions.

### Remarkable Help by Data Analysis Explained

In this way, I analyzed the data on the basis of qualitative approach which is appropriate for this study to analyze the data to discover the new knowledge and concluded it with my own personal reflection. It has also helped me to partake in discussion based on the cases and the themes that are generated. So on the basis of the cases in the narrative form and the themes; I have concluded the summary, conclusions and the implications of the study.

## Credibility: Addressing Trustworthiness of the Study

There are no any statistical tests for significance in qualitative studies. According to Gay and Airasian (2000), education research is conducted to provide trustworthy information regarding educational problems and their explanation (as cited in Koul, 2008). As a phenomenological case study researcher, I maintained credibility in each step of my research. I used prolonged engagement, thick description and member checking and peer debriefing to enhance the credibility of my research.

Prolonged Engagement: Advantage of : Prolonged engagement is spending longer time in the study area. It helps to develop the patterns and relationships of meaning with the participants (Moustaas, 1994). The natural situation and interview in their own area, has been maintained has helped me to understand and implement the experiences of children during the armed conflict and their situation at present.

I spent long time in the field in order to gather high quality data by exploring their experiences of education during and after the conflict and their present situation. Until I couldn't fulfill the purpose of my study and data saturation, I spend time with the participants in the field. The natural setting has helped me to understand their own phenomenon of the experiences.

## Thick Description

I have tried to gather rich and thick description of the experiences of the participants. "The case study approach makes use of multiple methods of data collection such as: Interviews, document reviews, archival records. It also directs and participant observations and subsequently 'thick descriptions' of the phenomena under study" (Yin, 2003). Holloway (1997) also said, "Thick description refers to the detailed account of field experiences in which the researcher makes explicit, the patterns of cultural and social relationships and puts them in context" (p. 154). Thus, I have tried to pay attention to the contextual details of the participants of my study and interpretation in their social context.

## Subtitles of Altering and Interpretations

Thick descriptions help to carry out the findings and provide the access to the researcher to the subtleties of altering and several interpretations (Walsham, 2005). This has helped me to transport readers to the setting and maintain the social relationship. I have also continued rigorous techniques and methods of gathering high-quality data and analyzing those data, making meanings of it and understanding the phenomena observing what they do, conversing what they say, and interpreting the situations as quoted by Carspecken (2001). So to generate the thick descriptions, I tried to maintain my words, gestures, postures as the participants had to make it in a natural setting. Therefore, it has been a vehicle to communicating the holistic picture of the experiences of the children.

## Member Checking: Ascertainment of Accuracy

Member checking is a process of getting feedback from the participants of the study. It helps to "determine the accuracy of the qualitative findings through taking the final report or specific descriptions or themes back to participants and determining whether these participants feel that they are accurate" (Creswell, 2003, p. 196). An ongoing dialogue regarding my interpretations of the informant's reality and meanings have ensured the true value of the data.

## Member Checking: A Critical Technique

Lincoln and Guba (1985) reflect member checking into the findings as "the most critical technique for establishing credibility" (p. 314). Member-checking has helped me to determine the accuracy of the qualitative findings. This is "through taking the final report or specific descriptions or themes back to participants and determining whether these participants feel that they are accurate" (Creswell, 2014, p. 201). I met and talked with the participants three times in order to know whether their information was right or they want to change or add anything related any interview question.

## Peer Debriefing: Ascertainment of Information Credibility

Peer debriefing is another technique to ensure the credibility of the information. It helps to maintain the precision and exactness of the field details (Creswell, 2003). So to regulate the quality standard of my research work, I conducted peer debriefing with my friend who was from the same background. I also shared the research process, interview, discussions, findings, conclusions, summary, conclusions and implications. In this regard, Creswell further added that this process involves locating a person (a peer debriefs) who reviews and asks questions about the qualitative study so that the account will resonate with people other than the researcher.

## Multiple Conversations with Particpants

The iterative data collection and analysis process has generated multiple conversations with participants and with my knowledgeable peers. So, "the participants of the resulted in meeting, the criteria of checking back with the people studied earlier to ensure credibility" (Neely & Tech, 2005, p. 81). In order to prove the quality standard in my research, I also discussed with my colleagues about my findings and conclusions.

## Ethical Considerations

Ethical issue in research is one of the important aspects in conducting the research. Anderson (1998) emphasized that, "all studies which involve people should consider ethical issues and responsibility of the individual researcher to see that any risk which may affect the community or the individual involved in the study, is minimized" (p. 81). It is believed that research design always needs to reflect careful attention to the issue embodied in research. McMillan and Schumacher (2001), highlighted "ethical guidelines include informed consent, deception, confidentiality, anonymity, harm, privacy and others" (p. 240). Keeping this in mind, I also negotiated and made consent with all my participants to voluntarily participate in the research.

## Points of Ethnics to be Considered

In accordance with the ethical guidelines issued by the university's research committee, being ethical meant that I had to be constantly in touch with my own values regarding trust, confidentiality, harm, deception and consent while considering the overall welfare of my research participants.

## Nothing is Concealed: Open Hearted Contacts

Being a qualitative researcher, to ensure their rights, I made it clear that my research was only an academic piece and it was not to earn any capital. I very honestly and clearly explained to them the objectives and nature of my research and requested them for the consent beforehand; I told them clearly that they had the rights to withdraw at any time without giving me any reason. Also, I informed them about data collection tools and activities as suggested by Creswell (2003). Then, I requested them to participate in the interviews.

## Winning Confidence of Participants

In addition, my participants were fully assured that no harm and no hurt in any way would come to them due to their participation in this research. All participants were assigned pseudonyms like Sarada, Mahadev, Khim and Radhika to ensure their identities remained confidential. They were guaranteed that no identifying information would be included in the study. Furthermore, all participants of my study, were also assured that the information they provided would be used only to fulfill the objectives of the research. During the entire research, I also took under consideration, their sensitivity in regards to age, ethnicity, gender, culture, religion, language and, socio-economic status. I also made sincere efforts to honestly interpret and report my findings. Besides these, I also followed the process of "member checks" (Richards, 2003) whereby I showed the complete transcripts to the research participants and directly obtained feedback from them.

## Summary of the Chapter

In this chapter, I discussed my philosophical stand points and assumptions on which I stood and shed light on the world of methodological knowledge based on my topic. And, this chapter also outlined the research design and described the research procedures in a great detail. A qualitative approach was adopted in an attempt to explore the experiences and coping adversities during the period of ten years armed conflict and post conflict situation in Nepal by interpreting the understandings, values, experiences, opinions and behaviours of my participants.

## A Preclude to Acts Performed

Moreover, the research design also focused on in-depth interview to explore the experiences of my research participants because this method was appropriate for studying the ways in which the research participants in this study experienced their education during the conflict period and coping adversities in post conflict situation. This chapter also stated the data collection and analysis procedures. To mention the trustworthiness of the study, quality standards were also presented. Finally, I made my effort to ensure the integration of ethical considerations into the research process.

# 4

# Experience of School Children on their Education and Life During Ten Years Armed Conflict

## An Introduction of Activities Done

In this chapter, I have presented the analysis of data gathered through interview with the participants. The collected data were recorded in an audio recorder and field notes. Then the data were transcribed and interpreted to seek meaning out of the data. This chapter started with a brief introduction of the participants, family background and parent's socio-economic condition and thus, it presented their academic experiences during the time of ten years armed conflict. Finally, I have summarized my understandings and then drew the theme.

## Sarada: A Victim of Social Exclusion

Sarada B.K. (pseudonym) is a participant of this study. There are mainly two reasons behind selecting Sarada as one of the participants for this study. First, she was a school going child who was under the age of eighteen during ten years armed conflict. She experienced exclusion in school and society and thus, participated in the ten years armed conflict. So, I wanted to explore her experiences on education during the period of ten years armed conflict and afterwards. Second, in the course of selecting the participant for interview for this study, I visited the local community of Gorkha district where the local leaders recommended that Sarada would be the best participant to get the information for my research. So, I am delighted to choose Sarada as an extreme case to see the children's education experiences during the period of ten years' armed conflict.

With the help of a local leader, I contacted Sarada on her cell phone and introduced myself and shared about my purpose. I requested her to manage some time to share her schooling experiences during the time of ten years conflict. Then, she accepted my request and provided me with the date, time and place to meet her.

## Sarda: A Village Woman

As per the telephone conversation, I went to meet Sarada at her home on the given time and date. When I reached her house and inquired whether she was inside or not; then an old woman came outside and told me that Sarada had gone to the field to cut the grass so I had to wait some hours for her. I then, sat in the yard and started to look around her house. Her house was surrounded by field. It was made of mud and had a thatched roof. There were small plants of maize in the field which looked very beautiful. Then I phoned her and she told that she reached near to her house. When she arrived, she looked tired as she was carrying a heavy load of grass in her basket. Her clothes were wet by sweat and somewhere they were also torn. She looked simple and any effect of modern society on her appeared absent in full.

## Question-Answer Session Began

After sometime, we sat on the veranda and introduced each other. At the same time, her mother brought some roasted maize and whey. I asked her who worked in the field to grow maize plants. She said it was her mother and herself. And, I began asking her my intended questions.

## Sources of Livelihood and other Details

Sarada was permanently from Taranagar VDC, ward number eleven of Gorkha District. When I asked her to say about her family background and the professions, her family members were engaged in, she said that she was from a marginalized lower caste poor family, known as Dalit. She had six members in her family including parents. Among the siblings, she was the oldest daughter. It was known that she had to care for her younger brothers and sisters because her parents were engaged in labor work in the field. That means, her parent's profession was to do the labor in rich people's work because, they were landless and had no other options to be engaged in their own land. So, her family depended on their 'laborer' occupation as a means of livelihood over the years. Her parents had worked in fewer wages in upper castes (i.e. Brahmins/Ksatriya) people. And it was hardly adequate to feed their family.

## Discriminated for Being a Dalit: Past and Present Experiences

After listening about her family background, I was caught by reminiscence of the livelihood of Dalit people in my village namely, Lumle. I had also observed similar conditions of Dalit people in Lumle during my childhood. I experienced that the so-called elite and upper castes people had used Dalits in their labor work at a cheap/low salary. They used the Dalit people as a servant and not a human being (*Gadhalai bharee bokaaye jasari*). I had seen that the Dalit people of Lumle were engaged more than 16 hours a day without rest but still they had not enough food at their home. They were hardly able to survive. I had some friends who were from the Dalit community in my schooling age. They were compelled to leave school even in the midsession and got involved to labor work and joined their parents' work. Since their parents' meager earning was not sufficient to look after the entire family, the children also had to go for wage labors. According to the report of the International Dalit Solidarity Network, (IDSN, 2015), Dalit children parents did not understand the importance of education and they forced their elder children especially girls to care for younger siblings and do house chores while parents work. So it can be said that Dalit households do not have the right environment for their children to purse studies.

## Description of Schooling Life

She said that she was as lucky as she got a chance to go school despite being a member of Dalit family. She was not able to say anything when I asked her about who created that opportunity. She only said that she got the chance to get enrolled in a school being a single kid in her family (at that time her young brother and sister were not born). Sarada was fourteen years and was studying in grade seven when the conflict was at pick. Her school was located in the next village. This was located in a remote area and required a lengthy walk. So to reach there, she should walk around one hour. She mostly had upper caste friends in her classroom. Only two boys from her community there and she was also a lonely girl from her community. Except those two boys, she never got the help of other friends in her class. So, it can be said that children of Dalit families were vulnerable and often discriminated even in their formal schooling. Due to the economic backwardness, their access to education is very poor and a significant numbers of Dalit school age children are forced to leave school. Even if their family allow them to attend school rather than work with the family, the parents are usually unable to buy uniforms, books and stationery for them (Dahal, 2002). So, they do not get different opportunities and becomes drop out shortly.

Even being a Dalit family member, she had got a chance to go to school and was able to get upgraded to grade eight from grade seven. But being a Dalit student, she had faced the discrimination and abuse and sometimes, she often stigmatized and thought to drop out of school. According to Sarada, students from the upper caste backgrounds behaved negatively in the classrooms and in such situation, teachers either stayed silent on it or also behaved negatively. She remembered:

### Sarada's Grievances

One day, it was lunch time and we were playing in the ground and our all teachers were eating their Tiffin. Unknowingly, I reached to touch the water bottle of our teacher (who taught us Nepali). It happened when I was running to meet my friend. He immediately caught me and started give blows with a stick in front of all teachers and my friends. I begged and requested him to forgive me for my unknowing mistake. He never listened to my concern about study afterwards, and also indirectly or directly started to discriminate me, such as neglecting, repeated blaming, and labeling as a weak performer (for being a Dalit), which made me too much frustrated. Sometimes we three, two Dalit boys and I, were segregated in the classroom. Neither the teachers cared, nor did our classmates. Our classmates who were from the upper castes, also behaved like teachers, they had a team except us. They never let their Tiffin be touched by us. If we mistakenly touch it, they would throw their Tiffin even though they were hungry. By this way, we were behaved like an animal even in the same class with the same teacher. (Field note, 20 February, 2015)

### Reminiscence of My Own Schooling

I remembered the day of my schooling when I listed the experience of Sarada. In grade ten, I was the first boy (standing first in terms of merit) and Govinda B.K. (pseudonym) was the second boy (standing second in terms of merit) in my class. While I had any confusion about any questions, then the teacher would happily teach me even out of school time but if Govinda asked his question in the school time, then the teacher would behave obnoxiously. The teacher always said to Govinda "What will you do after passing the SLC? After all, you have to plough the field though how much and how well you read." So, Govinda was denied of asking any questions in our class but was able to maintain the second position in the class whatever were the attitudes and behaviour of the teachers and other friends towards him.

It means that Dalit students were separated even in their classroom by the teachers, students and even administration. Human Rights Watch (HRW, 2007) also describes teachers as they are the one who declared that the Dalit students can't learn unless they are punished. So in the case of Sarada, if Dalit student make some minor mistakes, they had to face corporeal punishment, which was not the case for other students.

## Atrocity Inflicted on Dalits

The Dalits were denied of access to school water supplies, were not allowed to touch the lunch of other friends, segregated in the classroom and forced to perform manual scavenging on and around school premises. In addition, the Dalit children face discriminatory attitudes from the community as a whole, in particular from higher caste members who perceive education for Dalits as a threat to village hierarchies and power relations. They thought that if they provided the Dalits with education, one day they would be able to grasp power and their (upper castes peoples) position would be lost. So the non-Dalits do not want to provide any academic opportunity to the Dalit people and their children. The indirect discrimination by teachers, community people and school administrative staff by neglecting them, blaming, labeling of the Dalit students in academic performance all leads to social exclusion, irregular presence in classroom, less attention in studies, less involvement in school activities, not performing well, drop outs and failure (Bishwokarma, 2010). So it can be said that neither the school created an academic environment for the Dalit students nor did the community do so.

## Poverty

The family members of Sarada suffered from hunger and poverty. They had no other source of income than labor. They used to get low wages which was very limited for food and had no money for other needs like education, health and etc. Due to lack of money, lots of poor people faced death. It was similar in Sarada's family. In this regards, she recalls her childhood experience as:

It was the time of summer; my younger sister had suffered from seasonal disease. Without treatment at home, she becomes more serious day by day because of not having money. My parents were hurried to get money from elsewhere for her treatment but could not get even a single hundred rupees. Nobody of this village people believed our family. Due to cause of poverty, we could not hospitalize my sister and she cries died. (Field note, 20 February 2015)

## Multiple Consequences of Poverty

So, due to poverty, many families lose their life. Getting education is the great achievement in this context. Many parents merely cannot afford to send their children to school and are dependent on their workforce to safeguard the survival of the family (Bishowkarma, 2010). But many of them are dying because of the extreme poverty. They could recover if they have money but forced to kill themselves and the other living family members also were forced to see the death of relatives. In that miserable situation, she was hardly able to reach to school.

## Political Motivation

One day, while she reached school, she saw a dance program and the dancers were in army dress. At first, she was frightened and started thinking who were they and why were they dancing in school? After the dance, one speaker delivered a speech and he was telling about their agenda and their interest of conducting this program in her school. Then she came to know that they were the CPN (Maoist). After that, she moved near the CPN (Maoist) cadres to know about them. And she asked in details about them and told about herself in detail too. Then, one of the CPN (Maoist) cadres said that he was busy then and promised to come to her house later.

## Political Aspiration Sprouted

Next day the person, who had promised to come her house, came and she had introduced him with her family members. After they had meal, he started to talk but due to the cause of illiteracy and lack of political awareness, her parents were not able to understand what he was talking about but she was hardly able to understand what he told. He talked about the social exclusion, domination and its liberation through his party's revolution. She became more interested to know about his party and its political agenda. As per her request, he explained and provided her some books and materials for further reading. After that, she read these all documents with enthusiasm. Then, it made her more eager to comprehend about the ongoing CPN (Maoist) revolution. Neupane (2003) emphasized that the social and political agenda of the CPN (Maoist) motivated the school children especially from the socially excluded and marginalized community to get involved in the armed conflict even though they were below 18 years. And she herself tried to meet them and got more information day by day. As being a Dalit girl, she was more motivated to know about the CPN (Maoist) agenda against the caste based discrimination, untouchability and poverty. Furthermore, she found it interesting that the CPN (Maoist) party had given the priority on these issues and started the revolution for the liberty of those people who were socially excluded and oppressed.

## Discrimination Inserted in Cognition

After reading the materials which were provided to her by the CPN (Maoist) cadre, she started to remember her daily life where she experienced discrimination. Being a member of the marginalized community, she had faced several types of discriminations in her family and society from the elites and upper castes peoples. Sometimes, she had to stand for a long time in queue untouchably to fill the water and then get the chance to fill the water only after the upper castes women filled their pots. Similarly, she had seen the death of her younger sister because of poverty. She was much frustrated with the behaviour of her teachers, classmate and school administration. Thus, she thought to leave her schooling and joined the CPN (Maoist) movement to get liberty from such discriminations (as she was tempted by the cadres and the documents). Bhattachan and Webster (2005) have also highlighted that the root cause of involvement in the conflict was the social exclusion, poverty and discrimination.

The voices of the affected girl with regards to, what she had felt and experienced are highlighted below:

## Voices of Affected Sarada- A Girl

I belong to a marginalized lower caste poor family. My family has to work for rich people for more than 16 hours a day but still we do not have enough food at home. It was really a difficult task to solve hand to mouth problem. We never get access to resources in the community as well as the state. My family had never had the access to hospital, communication and other development aspects. I was feeling discriminated in the school by the teachers and friends. My friends even did not sit near me and share their lunch because I was from the lower caste. So I thought it was all because of the exploiting system of the state; therefore, I joined the CPN (Maoist) to fight against the system, and to establish a new state with equal distribution of all resources among us. (Field note, 20 February, 2015)

### Radical Cause for Joining CPN (Maoist)

It seems that the existing social system led her to join in the CPN (Maoist) revolution. Because of being a Dalit family member, Dalit students face many problems (Bishowkarma, 2010) and she had also faced many problems even in formal education as a student. For her liberation, she thought that she needed to join in the CPN (Maoist) revolution. According to her interview, she was just fourteen years old at the time of joining the CPN (Maoist) party. And she said that she was unknown about child rights and conventions which insisted on protecting the child rights and advocating stopping of recruiting (as CPN –Maoist cadres) children under the age of eighteen. She was searching the way for liberty because of being an affected of social discrimination. So, it supplied more enlightenment to her to be a revolutionary.

### Involvement in Political Activities

Sarada worked in Student Union at first i.e. CPN (Maoist) s' sister student organization– All Nepal National Independent Students Union (Revolutionary) for two years and then she was shifted to PLA. She had worked as an active fighter in the major attacks several times. Regarding this, she shared:

## Experiences in Politics

I had almost forgotten my family during that period. Friends and party was everything for me and I had promised to fight against the system, and to establish a new state with equal distribution of all resources to all on the basis of their demand and to promote right to education to all the children by shifting the trend from bourgeois (traditional) to janawadi (popular). (Field note, 21 February, 2015)

Similarly, it was argued by Devkota (2014) that our social structure created the gap between the peoples of our society on the bases of caste, race and economic conditions. As a result, rich people are richer and poor people are poorer. So children who were under the age of eighteen were discriminated on the bases of caste, ethnicity and religion. It was oriented to them that they were fighting for the country first and then only their families. They were ready to lose everything for the liberation of social exclusion and discrimination in their society.

## My Reflection on Factors Causing Discrimination

After analyzing Sarada's case, I realized that multi-ethnicity, caste differences and inequalities are crucial aspects in the social, political, cultural and economic structures within Nepal (Shakya, 2006). People are discriminated as Dalit, poor and marginalized. It was part of the CPN (Maoist) agenda to eliminate discrimination on the basis of caste and ethnicity, rich and poor as it prevents discriminated people and those from marginalized group from gaining equal access in the society. These structural inequalities provided a fertile ground for the CPN (Maoist) to encourage members of the lower castes, disparate ethnic groups, and school going children to participate in Ten years armed conflict. So social exclusion, poverty and CPN (Maoist) political agenda led the school children to quit school and join the CPN (Maoist) movement even though, they were under the age of eighteen.

## Mahadev: The Cost of Being Different

Mahadev Shrestha (pseudonym) is another participant in this study. He is from Mosel -1 of Gorkha district. I think his life could be of interest to my research as his education and daily life was affected by the ten years armed conflict in Nepal. I knew about him from Ram Shrestha (pseudonym) who was working in an NGO in the field of child education. As said by Ram, Mahadev was under the age of eighteen while he was harmed by the ten years armed conflict. I also came to know that Mahadev was affected by the CPN (Maoist) party.

## Process to meet and Conduct Interview

For my study, I took his cell number from Ram Shrestha and contacted him. He informed me that he could visit me only on Saturday because he was engaged in a job. After six hours travel from Kathmandu by bus, I reached Gorkha headquarters in his given time. At that time Mahadev had come to the bus station to meet me.

## A Virgin Introduction

When we met at the station, he greeted me and asked if we could take tea together. Then we went to a nearby tea shop and started our conversation. I told him about the purpose of visit and reason for choosing him in my study. He easily accepted my request. In the evening, he requested me to go to his room and we went there. While he was preparing food, I observed the condition of his room where there were very few things needed for him. For example, there was only one single bed, old mattress and a few cooking utensils. There was a picture of a man of around forty years. I asked him whose picture that was. He replied seriously that it was his father's picture. After we had meal, we again talked for some time before going to bed.

## Inquiry About Family, Profession and Schooling

During our conversation, I wanted to know a little more closely about his family. Then, he shared that he had six members in his family. By profession, his father was a secondary level English teacher at a government school in his own village. Being a son of a literate person, Mahadev had got good academic environment at his home. He told me that his father was always concerned about his childrens' study and career. When he got some leisure time, he would teach his kids and sometimes play with them. This meant, he gave the first priority to his kids' education. As a result, Mahadev did never hold the second position in his academic life. He was able to uphold the first position from the beginning of his academic journey.

## A Specific Social Impression

As a son of a teacher, Mahadev got the love and care of other teachers as well in his school. All subject teachers motivated and encouraged him in their classes. They mostly cared him more than other students and passed the daily academic progress report to his father. Similarly, his classmates also wanted to sit with him in the class and wanted to play with him. He got family-like environment at school, too.

## Victim of Unlawful Killing

Mahadev shared about the accident in which he had lost his father. He was killed because of having different political ideology as a teacher and not paying levy to the party. At that time, forces from the government of Nepal and the CPN (Maoist) targeted civilians with impunity, frequently accusing individuals of politically supporting their enemy. United Nations Office of the High Commissioner for Human Rights (2012) in Conflict Report, Nepal has also identified the reasons behind the killings of the professionals like teachers by the CPN (Maoist). This report also highlighted that unlawful killings were also performed against enemy combatants and nationals who were against them and also used to be under their control. He shared:

## Episode Highlighted

It was the mid-evening of the winter season, we three (I (myself), my brother and sister) were doing homework with the help of our father and our mother was cleaning the dishes. In the meantime, nearly 6-8 people wearing masks entered our room. I was afraid seeing them. I went near my mother and watched their activities. Among them, one tall man requested our father to go with them for some inquiry about school but my father replied them to ask there. Irrespective of my father's request they forced him to go out and at last, he went out with them. When my father was about to go out, he said that *"ramro saga padh hai chora ma ekchin uncle haru saga guff garera aauchhu"* (Read nicely my son, I will come back soon after talking with the uncles). We could not sleep and my mother was crying the whole night. I neither could manage my textbooks and copies nor could complete my homework. My brother and sisters were taken into the room by my brother. I and my mother waited for the arrival of my father for a long time. I did not remember when I slept. I used to sleep with my father but that day, I was alone. (Field note, 1 March, 2015)

He was continuously telling his story and I was silently writing his story on my note book. I had no words to ask him, so I was just listening to him. He continued:

## Piteous Listeners to Episode

In the morning, I found myself in the same place where I was studying. My mother was doing some household chores. I asked her if father had arrived but she said 'no' in a weepy voice. In the meantime, our neighboring uncle and grandmother came into our house. They seemed sad with a gloomy face. For some minutes, they were speechless. By seeing them, my mother was more serious and again started crying with a loud voice and asked what had happened to her husband. It was very difficult to just produce a sound. The situation was very piteous. Grandmother held my mother and I was in the lap of the uncle. Again my mother asked them about the situation of our father and they told us he was no more in the world. The dead body of our father was lying in the field of that uncle. After listening to this, mother got fainted and I also couldn't remember what happened after that. Still I cannot believe that it was real and I wish it was only a dream. (Field note, 1 March, 2015)

## My Condition as a Mute Listener

Mahadev was sharing his experiences and I was just keeping notes, I was speechless too. Tears were like the clouds in the sky, which were ready to fall down to clear the sky. The situation seemed like, he got someone to share his feelings and I was there to solve the problem.

He was looking so grim while he was telling about miserable incident of his father. I had no any words to express sympathy at that moment. I was just listening to him. He was continuously telling his entire life story after his father was killed. Remembering that day and the time, he had survived in the absence of his father; he was almost mad and scared. He caught my fingers and said:

> I get nightmares all the time. I see those people coming and kidnapping my families. I am still afraid that something similar will happen again. Those people who killed my father, could come at any time and intimidate us as they want to settle the case without any inquisition. I've been receiving threats from them that the same thing can happen to me if I do inquiry with the state security men. I used to have suicidal feelings in the beginning. But I thought, if I kill myself, my family will also die. As the eldest child of the family, I am living because of the love for my family. (Field note, 1 March, 2015)

He was very upset in saying all those things. I tried to ask about the incident that happened on that night when his father was taken away. In this respect, he added:

> We searched for our father but got the dead body. After the rituals, we tried to search for the person who had come that night but couldn't. It was at the peak hour of the conflict and no one was there to speak a single word for our help. We couldn't get justice from anyone. There was also another danger that if we report the case to the police then; they could arrest us any time. Thinking that the CPN (Maoist) would again repeat the same accident if they knew that we have reported the police, we could not report it. So we remained silent. After some time, we got to know from the teacher of the school that the CPN (Maoist) party has asked some amount of money because my father was in support of some other party. He had provided some amount but it was not exactly how much the CPN (Maoist) party had demanded. So my father became their target and was killed. (Field note, 2 March, 2015)

## A Buzz of Crime Everywhere

At this time, the CPN (Maoist) often executed civilians publicly to create fear, while the government routinely eliminated its perceived enemies through enforced disappearances, IHRC (2013). Not only CPN (Maoist), both sides committed torture and severe beatings as well as rape and other forms of sexual violence. This report furthermore states that the perpetrators carried out these crimes in particularly violent ways, and families often experienced multiple incidents of abuse and even killed. And after the death of a breadwinner, there also usually placed a heavy burden on families and especially on elder children of the family. They left the school and became a breadwinner of the family.

## Struggle for Survival

After that mishap in his family, he had appealed to the government to investigate and find the truth in his father's death. But the government could not officially declare the reality behind his father's death even after a decade of the incident.

## Indecisiveness

Sometimes, he thought to shift his family into a safe place, where he could feel fearless and secured. He wanted to forget the dreadful accident. But due to the cause of economic crisis, he could not migrate from his birthplace where he had lost his father. He was bound to live in that place even though he had an interest of migrating since his family had much grievances and the economic burden when his father was killed.

## Some are Schooling Days: A Flood of Grievances

It is obvious that in the Nepali society, the leader of the family is mostly the male member. In this case also his father was the key person for their survival. He was the family's breadwinner. So when Mahadev lost his father, his mother obviously faced the crisis. In this case, his mother was facing difficulties to manage the expenses for the children's studies and clothes when the CPN (Maoist) killed her husband, IHRC (2013). And then, Mahadev had to discontinue his studies in private school because of the poverty. He, his brother and sister had left that school and joined the public school. Similarly, in the absence of his father, he was bound to do agriculture activities and all labor work at the age of 16. Later, he left the school as he could not attend regularly because of his full time engagement in the field. But he helped his brother and sister in their study. He said that he was helpless and was like an orphan. He added, "My uncle and aunt were in a good condition but they did not help us. They even tried to kick us out of the house".

## Social Compassion: Zero to Victims

Furthermore Mahadev said that after his father's death, everyone started hating him and his family rather than supporting them. Similarly they were excluded in many cultural functions. He further added that his agricultural land was captured by his relatives as he was small and no one was there to help him. The relatives and community people also added the sufferings to his family.

## My Reflection: Children in Topsy-turvy Situation

Through the story of Mahadev, it can be said that school going children were affected by the CPN (Maoist) revolution. After their parents were killed by the CPN (Maoist) party, they were forced to leave school and get into domestic labor at a time when they should be attending school. Similarly, children have been adversely affected in many ways by the armed conflict in Nepal. They and/ or their parents have been killed or made disabled. They have been psychologically and economically traumatized (IHRC, 2013) like

Mahadev. Their education has been interrupted. They have been displaced from their education. Their educational development has been affected as a direct result of the armed conflict.

## Khim Bahadur: An Eye for an Eye

When I met the first participant (Sarada) for my study and shared my purpose then she recommended that Khim Bahadur Kumal (pseudonym) who was from Taranagar VDC ward number eleven of Gorkha, would be another participant. She shared that Khim Bahadur was also under the age of eighteen and affected by the conflict. He was forced to join in the CPN (Maoist) movement even though, he was a school going child. Social exclusion and poverty was the main reason for him to join the CPN (Maoist) party.

## Systematic Meeting

Then Sarada called him and shared the purpose. After that she told him that I would be calling him and sharing the details. He agreed to talk with me. Then Sarada gave me the contact number and I called him and explained him my purpose in details. We agreed to meet at Ten Kilo, way to Gorkha Bazar from Aabu Khaireni of Tanahun. I took a vehicle from Sarada's house and moved to Ten Kilo. I saw two/three people in the station. I was wondering which one was Khim Bahadur. When I just got off the vehicle, one person stood and looked around. I thought he might be my participant. I asked him if he was Khim Bahadur, he said he was and we exchanged Namastes. Then he requested me to go to his home and talk there in details. And we moved towards his home.

## Story of Another Participant

We sat on the Verandah and got ready to start our discussion. He offered me to take water. When I was drinking the water, suddenly, I saw a calendar hanging at the door. I saw some pictures in the calendar and went to see it. I saw that the calendar was about the killed and missing people of Kumal community, who were affected by the government's action. Then Khim Bahadur explained to me about the calendar and showed me the picture of his father in the list. It was about 4 o'clock. The school going students were returning from school. He shared showing the students that, some of them had lost their parents, some had lost their relatives, some had lost their brothers and sisters and some have still been disappeared. By listening to that, I came to know that the Kumals of that area were highly affected in the conflict. Up to this time, he had already prepared some foods to eat.

## How Courteous People Where There?

It was in the evening that we had started talking and the day was slowly turning to night. I was unknown where to stay. In the meantime, Khim Bahadur asked me if I have arranged the hotels to stay that night or not? I replied 'No'. Then, he requested me to stay at his home and adjust with whatever he has in his home. I couldn't ignore his hospitality. He prepared food for the night. I was also helping him and was trying to ask about the situation they faced during the conflict. After having food, he started to share what the exact situation before the conflict was, how he became the affected of the government when he was only a student.

Hence my third participant was Khim Bahadur Kumar. He was from Taranagar VDC ward number eleven of Gorkha. He had five members in his family. He was the youngest child in his family. As a family profession, his father was a farmer. But farming was not enough for their livelihood. So they had to work on others' houses and fields. And it was very difficult for them to fulfill, all demands of the family members. Due to this condition, Khim Bahadur's eldest brother was also unable to join the school. But luckily, Khim

Bahadur was sent to school as there were elders to look after the farm.

## Exclusion and Drop-out

He got the chance to join the school but the facilities needed for him were not provided so he had to struggle for it. Sometimes, his empty stomach did not help him to grasp the lessons taught at school. Due to the cause of extreme poverty, he had faced many challenges in his school. Therefore, he couldn't do better at school. Because of his weak performance he was not treated well. Neither the teachers nor the classmates cared him. The teachers used to give time to him but he was not ready to do as per the sayings of the teachers. So his teachers never asked any questions and consulted with him after that. Moreover, he was always scolded by his teachers as a dull student.

## Troubles One After Another?

Similarly, he was isolated by the classmates. He became lonely as his habit was different from others and no one was ready to make him a group member. His classmates never shared Tiffin with him. His friends had never seen his Tiffin so they did not share their Tiffin as well. He used to be alone during the recess. Even he had returned home sometimes at mid-day. Similarly Dalit children face inequitable insolences from fellow students and the community as a whole, in particular from upper caste members who perceive education for Dalits as a waste and a threat (Islam & Uddyog, 2011). This is linked to a perception amongst upper caste people that educated Dalits pose a threat to village hierarchies and power relations, and that Dalits are generally incapable of being educated .This perception of upper caste people has influenced their school going children and they also showed such behave in school what they learned at home and society. Khim not only faced such problem, he has also faced several problems like, not having good school dress, and other necessary materials like copies, pencils, books, etc for his study. He explained:

## Schooling Days

When I was trying to do my homework, I couldn't get copies. I asked my father to buy a copy but my father said that he would buy it next week when he might get his salary. I was so sad and didn't want to go to school but father compelled me to go to school. And the school teacher, who was not aware about my situation, punished me for my not doing the homework. Even a teacher said that if I don't have copies, then I have to leave the school. I felt very ashamed of this and started crying. I started to scold the god why he made us poor. As an average student in terms of academic performance, I sometimes, dreamt of not going to school but doing work and earn enough money. (Field note, 24 March ,2015)

## Extreme Poverty: Explained as Basic Reason

His feelings expressed the extreme poverty of his family and the situation how he was coping with the problems. He could not get much support from teachers, students and home as well in his study. So, day by day, he became less interested to go to school. And he was thinking of earning money using any effort. He severely regretted on why he was born into the poor family. He thought that it was better to work and earn money rather than go to school for study.

## Fear and Torture

His father used to share his pains and conditions of surviving with his neighbor. He was searching a condition from where he would get rid of poverty. He was roaming here and there in search of good job but it was very difficult to fulfill the basic demands of his family.

## Friends Also Turned Into Enemies

One day, when he went to his neighbor to ask for some loan for the study of his children, his neighbor suggested him to join the CPN (Maoist) party. His neighbor even added that the CPN (Maoist) party was the only one and emerging new political force which was in favor of the poor and needy people so his problem would also be solved through the revolution of that party. Then, his father decided to join the CPN (Maoist) party to eradicate the poverty and eliminate the gap between the rich and the poor. Then he left his home and became underground. After his father's underground life, Khim Bahadur's family faced extreme poverty day by day. His elder brother alone was unable to provide food for morning and evening.

## Bother Schooling and Manual Labour Together

Then he started to support his brother's work in the morning and in the evening and used to go to school during the day. But after the father's involvement in the CPN (Maoist) party, the state security force started to torture his family day by day (Gautam, 2007). His family was blamed as CPN (Maoist) supporter and punished when he was found working or in school. He remembered:

## Misuse of Abuse of Talent and Diligence

Around 20 people came to my house at around 6 am. They asked where my father was. I was afraid to talk with them but they asked me time and again and compelled me to talk with them. But my father was already underground and far from our home. They asked if we had hid our father. If we did not speak, they would kill us. They threatened us. At this time, I thought that the people were Nepal Army personnel. And they asked whether we had given food and shelter to the combatants or not. Among them, one of the soldiers slapped on my brother face three times as we were not answering. His face got swollen, and he screamed with pain. (Field note, 24 March, 2015)

## Threats and Suppression's Also Coercion

He further added, eight days later, the soldiers came to his house again at 7 am and again abused his brother. They asked several questions to him and his brother but they couldn't answer because of fear. At that time, they arrested his brother and put him into jail in the headquarters. He was physically and mentally tortured many times in jail. They kept him there for three months. After appealing to the politicians, and they in turn told the armies. After that, they released him. His brother was beaten harshly in jail. His family took him to the hospital for treatment. During the period of ten year armed conflict, children are regularly tortured by the state security force and police personnel for suspected CPN (Maoist) activity or in an attempt to gain information about CPN (Maoist) activities or to find the whereabouts their CPN (Maoist) parent (Watch List on Children and Armed Conflict, 2005).

## Revenge Against Barbarous Atrocities

He said that he was bound to join the Moist party even though he was under the age of fifteen because, it was his last option in order to remain alive from the state security force: i.e. Nepal Police, Nepal Army and Unified Command. The state security force used to raid their houses regularly, give physical torture to the members of his family, rape women and young girls in the society and torture them (WLCAC, 2005). So he said that he joined CPN (Maoist) Party after being tortured by the state force for the reason that his father was a CPN (Maoist) and away from them. His family even got physical tortures for supporting the CPN (Maoist) when they were underground by giving them shelter. Regarding this, he shared:

## Frequent Suppression and Tortures by the State

One night, I was studying in my room. A group of Nepal Army personnel came to my home and asked many questions to my mother and elder brother about my father who was a CPN (Maoist) cadre and away from home. They beat my brother cruelly; and my sister in law who was pregnant at that time came to rescue my brother. Two of the army raped her in front of me and beat her until she got unconscious. I was hiding myself in the room but watching all the brutal activities of that army. It was the situation which no one can tolerate and see. Anyone, who sees such activities would be a fighter in a moment. At that moment, I remembered that my father was fighting for these types of activities and I have to join it. So, I decided to join the CPN (Maoist) party to take revenge of that brutality. (Field note, 1 March, 2015)

## How Tough to See Atrocity Committed Before One's Eyes?

This kind of heart touching bitter reality still gives the scenario of that time and allows us to imagine how the people might have faced the conflict and its tentacles. Khim was studying in grade seven but his study became a hateful task for him by seeing such activities. He was the eyewitness of how the general people were being affected by the army force. For him, it was the age of school going and playing, enjoying with the friends but it turned out to have been the compulsion to join in the CPN (Maoist) movement as he couldn't bear any further torture. He started being a rebel. He left the house at the same moment. Not only Khim, there were big number of children recruitment when the state security force charged them as a CPN (Maoist) supporters and tortured them regularly (WLCAC,2005). Children felt unsecure to stay home and were involved in armed conflict even they were school student.

## Search for Another Rival Forces

At first he did not know where to go and whom to meet. He was roaming here and there. After walking for about an hour, he remembered one person who used to come with his father in his house. His father had shown him the house of that person so that they could communicate and know the condition of his father. So, he went to that house. Unfortunately, he was not in the house. He waited and waited, after some time that person came and he shared all the activities that had happened in his house and he wanted to join in the CPN (Maoist) movement in order to take revenge. Then that person took him in the place where the CPN (Maoist) was conducting a program and he was welcomed with a red salute. According to the report of International Committee of the Red Cross (2009), such activities forced many children join armed conflict like Khim Bahadur. It means that context and situation led them to leave school and compelled them to be involved in the battle even if they were under the age of eighteen.

## Training to Take Revenge

He said that he was too young to fight and even to lift the gun. But later, he practiced and became perfect. He had a dream that if he would be able to kill the army force it would be a great tribute to his family members. After one year, he met his father and shared the entire incident that had happened in his home. And they two promised to end such types of activities in the society through the revolution. Then they departed for doing their own task as assigned. After some months he got the news from the party that his father got martyrdom and was announced as martyr. This news shocked him and he thought that he was the only one to earn respect for his family through revolution. Again one day, he got a letter that his brother was kidnapped accusing him to be a terrorist. But it has still been unknown about his whereabouts and who had kidnapped him. He was affected by forced disappearance and the family is still waiting for his return. Now he has courage and power to fight against such activities.

## Risks and Injuries Coped With

He was injured in 'Myagdi attack' and could not run away to be safe and arrested by the security force. After that, he was kept in jail of Kaski. The security force gave him mental and physical torture in jail. He was seriously injured by the security person's punishment but could not get treatment. After the CPA, he got released from the jail and was able to return his own home. But he saw the pitiful situation of his house. No one was there to take care of his ill mother. Then he started to look after his mother.

## My Reflection: How Does Retaliation Arise

The reasons why children participate in the ten years conflict are numerous. According to the story of Khim, he joined the revolution because the government security men constantly harassed his family for supporting the CPN (Maoist) party or for the sheltering them overnight and providing food to them (**IHRC,2013**). Similarly, he wanted to take revenge with the security forces for doing unethical social harassment with his family members.

## Radhika: Unheard Voices of Patriotism

The fourth participant of this study was Radhika Thapa (pseudonym) and she is from Mosel 2 Bhatta Gau of Gorkha district. I got to know her with the help of Ram Shrestha (pseudonym) who is a human rights advocator and working for National Human Rights Commission. As told by Ram, he worked at Gorkha district before one year and he became familiar with Radhika during that period. From Ram, I came to know that she was a conflict affected child from the CPN (Maoist) side. At that time, she was a school student and ten years armed conflict ruined her schooling so I think she was a suitable participant for my study and I decided to meet her.

## Initiatives Taken

For that day (2015-02-18), I had requested Ram to come to my residency for lunch. And as per my request, he came. While having lunch, I explained to him about my research purpose. After listening about my purpose, he gave me Radhika's details. And I thought that she would be an important participant for my study while I listened about her. Then I took her contact number from Ram and called her.

## Participant's Curiosity to Meet

Once I shared the purpose of calling her, she was ready to meet me. As per the telephone talk, I went to meet Radhika at her house on the given time and date. When I reached her home, there were four people who were cutting the wood and making some planks. Then I asked them about Radhika and got answer that she was inside home. She was preparing some food while I entered her home. And I told her about myself and she requested me to wait for some minutes. She said that she needed some time.

## Scene Nearby Participants Residence

I moved outside her home and started to see the technique of cutting the wood. One man was on the top of the ladder and other one was down the ladder. They were cutting the wood in one hundred degree shape. I got the real application of mathematics in this activity and remembered the teaching class of mathematics of my teacher. In the meantime, I saw a damaged shed for buffalos near her home. And I came to know that the workers were cutting wood to rebuild the buffalo shelter.

## A Fair Entertainment

After some times, Radhika came with a mat and put it on the side of the yard. She requested me to sit and carried some food and wished me to take. Then, I had also requested her to eat together. And we started eating and talking at the same time.

## Session for Raising Questions

At first, I asked her to tell about her background, their condition and her academic performance during the period of ten years armed conflict. She told me that she was from Mosel ward no. 7, Gorkha district. She had a joint family where 15 family members were living together with grandfather and grandmother. Her father was the eldest son with one brother (her uncle) and six sisters. She added, "My uncle was physically disabled and we needed to take care of him. My father had colossal responsibilities to take care of whole families." She further added that through her father's lower positioned government job (Nepali army); they were hardly able to survive. Education was not the first priority in their family.

## Arrogance and Revelry Inserted

Father's involvement was directly seen in her academic performance, she was never counted as an intelligent student in the class. And she got less caring of her teachers and talented friends in her education. It seems that she hardly get support from home and school in education. And she herself never gave more time for study; she spent more time on house work to support her parents. There was no one to help her father except her mother, so she was also helping her mother in different household activities

## Professional Integrity and Death

She added that before the time of ten years armed conflict, her family was very happy despite being poor. When she was studying in grade 10(*2055 B.S.*), she and her family were directly affected by the ten years armed conflict. She tried to remember that day:

## Impact or Decade Long Conflict

In the early morning at around 5 a.m. on Baisakh 24, 2055, my father left home to go to Pokhara in order to join his duty. I also went along with him to the bus station. While we were walking through Dobhar which is at Tarkerabari Ward No. 7, Gorkha, suddenly a team of people appeared in front of us. They encircled my father and took him to a watercourse near that village. One woman, aged like my mother captured me, and tried to close my eyes and she beat me a lot and I started to cry. (Field note, 15 April 2015)

## "Pathos" in Explanation

Radhika, with tears rolling down her cheeks said that the people who had done such things were the CPN (Maoist). They have asked her father to leave the job of Nepalese army and join with them but he denied. She said that she was unknown that the CPN (Maoist) group has suggested her father several times to quit the job. She added that her father was one of the patriots of the nation so he was ready to die rather than surrendering.

## Barbarous Activities

According to Myers (2008), there are lots of incidents of killing and abusing from the security persons whatsoever they were in off time and even they were at home. In the same way, her father was killed when he was out of duty. She added that she had listened this kind of inhumanity action and the fight between the two parties but she was the real eyewitness of the incident. They had tried to convince her father several times on what would be the benefit when he would leave his job but he spoke against them. She concluded that this might be the main reason why they shot her father.

### Fearful Experience

Her voice was full of fear when she said that the CPN (Maoist) dragged him to the river and the corpse was thrown into the river. She was helpless and could not do anything at that movement. She could not even forgive herself that she was the eye witness of the death of her own father and she could do nothing. In this regards, she added "I am really troubled after my father's death. I don't even have any idea what to do or not to do. My heart and mind always think negatively, which makes me weaker and mad".

### Rules and Regulation – No nest or Null and Void

She felt pity on the rules and regulations of the nation. A fighter for the nation has given his life in the name of the nation. She could not control her while saying this. After the death of her father, her family moved everywhere to tell about the death of her father. They asked to punish the criminal at the national and international level. But could not get any support from anywhere. Then, they tried to go to the Supreme Court but it was not accessible by the citizens during the period of conflict, Gautam (2001). Unfortunately, their case was dismissed without proper investigation.

### Crisis of Guardianship

After her father's death, she faced a very big change in her life. She was the eldest child of her family and she had to handle all the work outside and inside the house, taking care of mother, young brothers and sister, land and household needs. Her two brothers were still young and studying. She added that she got sick and weak because of the tension and responsibility. In this regards, she said:

## Feeling Orphan Like

Whenever I go to check up my health, the doctor tells me that I have been suffering from chintarog [worries as disease]. I have been taking medicine. My mother has been also suffering from the same disease, the disease created by worry. She used to get fainted and I took her to different places in the course of her treatment. The doctor said that her disease was the source of her worries. Doctor has given me medicine to sleep. (Field note, 15 April 2015)

## Whole Some Sank in Shock

Her grandmother also got sick and could not get good treatment because of the poor economic status. The whole house was still in shock. She was trying herself to take care of the entire family but it was not useful. Everything became dry in her life that year. She remained unanswered when her sister and two small brothers asked about their father. She said, "The two brothers ask about father from time to time. This is the biggest tension to me and my mother. It is very hard for me to bear this."

## Media Reports

In this regards, the report of IHRC (2013) states that this is the never-ending pain for them and their family has undergone mental pain due to this problem and the mental pain has created other physical pains of convictism family in post conflict era of Nepal. The same situation is seen in Radhika's family. After the death of her father, she was away from the study. She herself became ill. Her mother and grandmother also suffered from illness. At the time of her father's death, she had passed the sent up examination and was preparing for the SLC examination. She failed in three subjects as she couldn't focus on her study. She had to read again and appear in the examination but she didn't get any chance to go to school again and study. She was more focused on the study of her brothers and sisters. She used to go to work with her mother which only will fulfill their daily requirement of basic needs.

## Experiences of Toughest Realities

She in an elegiac voice said that, "Sometimes it was very difficult for me and my mother to maintain the daily needs. We used to have fear on the festival that how to provide the small children as per their requirement". She added that she used to wish that there won't be any festival so that they could live a normal life. The society also didn't help them for their livelihood. So they were in a way isolated from the society. It was a long time that they have lost their father but still they are facing the scarcity on his absence. According to the report of Amnesty International (2013), it is stated that the government of Nepal is not able to hear and resolve the needs and expectations of thousands of affected. They are deprived of their rights even in post conflict situation whatever the government and political parties committed.

## My Reflection: Armed Conflict – ASCEAR to Humanity

The armed conflict has affected children of all ages especially schooling children through their family member's death. However, it has particularly affected school going children by disrupting their education and interfering with their access to educate. Some children have been removed from school to help at home like Radhika, as older member of the family have been killed in armed conflict. While a lot of them were in orphanages, a much bigger number was forced to work in dangerous conditions at brick kilns, quarries and wool spinning mills (Amnesty International Report, 2005).

Others had become domestic servants and doing labor in school going time even in schooling age.

## Cross Case Analysis

### *Commitments by Govt.*

The CRC was ratified by Nepal on September 14, 1990. Nepali government has the commitment to keep children away from becoming delinquent and affected. As an associate country of CRC, Nepalese government had ensured the guarantee of no any children shall be subjected to torture or other cruel, inhuman or degrading treatment or punishment. Although the political party's manifestos clearly included the commitment of the protection of child rights, the documents seem that the child rights will be protected and children will have good environment to get education.

## Commitments Proved False: Gross Violation of CRC

The interviews with the participants have concluded that practically, the commitment is not implemented. Both the government officials and the CPN (Maoist) shave heavily affected the school going children during the period of ten years armed conflict even if they were under the age of eighteen. Social discrimination, family involvement in the armed conflict and parent's death, etc. led the school going children to deprive of his\her liberty unlawfully or arbitrarily in Nepal during the period of ten years conflict. After taking interview with participant of this study, I came to know that the government and the rebel party (CPN -Maoist) broke the child convention and protection in Nepal during the era of ten years conflict. And neither the government nor the CPN (Maoist) party had respected the CRC and seen responsible to protect the right of the children. So, whatever the right to children was widely recognized in inter/national law, in practice it was often overshadowed by the state and the CPN (Maoist) party in ten years armed conflict.

## Table 1: Experiences of School Going Children

| Participant | Reasons of Not Getting Education | Involvement |
|---|---|---|
| Sarada | -Poverty<br>-Social Exclusion(Caste base discrimination)<br>-Teacher/student discrimination in school<br>-Political agenda of CPN (Maoist) party | -Recruit in CPN (Maoist) party<br>-Work as a member of CPN (Maoist) sister organization ANNSU(R)<br>-Join in fighter team(PLA) |
| Mahadev | -Different political ideology<br>- Father death<br>-breadwinner of family<br>-Enforce to join job<br>-Caring responsibility | -Responsible in house work<br>- Accountable in younger brothers and sister education<br>-Join job to fulfill basic need for family survival<br>-Join private institution as a part time student |
| Khim Bahadur | -Family involvement in CPN (Maoist) party<br>-State security regular harm in family<br>-Poverty<br>- Revenge | -Join in CPN (Maoist) party<br>-Became a fighter (PLA) |
| Radhika | -Father profession<br>-Father death<br>-Main responsibility as a senior member in family<br>- Asking justice<br>-Family caring | -Left the school<br>-Caring on family members<br>-Spend much time in house activities |

## Concluding Remarks on Sufferings of Participants

### *Ist Participant*

Sarada faced several kinds of social discrimination, caste based discrimination, gender based discrimination, poverty, domination from so called elites, upper castes people in her school, society, and community. She has seen the programs of CPN (Maoist) party where she has known about the political agenda of that party which was addressing the problems and discrimination that Sarada has faced. She was inspired by the ideas and was compelled to accept the agenda of the CPN (Maoist) party with the theme of change in the society and get freedom from that discrimination. The interest of Sarada was to participate in the programs of CPN (Maoist) party; she was made a member and later joined in PLA before the age of 18, though it was her school going age.

### *IInd Participant*

Similarly, Khim Bahadur was another affected. He was affected as his father was participating in the CPN (Maoist) party. He was tortured by the state security forces most of the time. He has seen the panic situation of his family members when his sister in law was raped and family members were beaten heavily but he was unable to do anything. From this moment he became an enemy of the state security forces and wanted to take revenge of the unsocial works of the security forces, he was unable to concentrate in education. There was no good environment for studying at home and in the surroundings. So he couldn't continue his education and joined in the CPN (Maoist) party.

### *IIIrd Participant*

Likewise, Mahadev was another affected but differently from the above situations. His father was a school teacher. His father was threatened and was asked money from the CPN (Maoist) party as he has different political ideology. He denied supporting them so he was killed. After the death of Mahadev's father, Mahadev was the one who has to support for his family and find the criminal of his father's death. His education was in shadow as he has other major responsibilities to perform in the family. He has to help his mother, provide education of small brothers and sisters, and provide sympathy to them. So he started working in an office and has little time and he joined for private education. The time which he has to spend on education with his family was destroyed by the death of his father and he was compelled to left education and does some income generating activities. After some time, he joined private institutions and continued part time education.

### *IVth Participant*

In the same way, Radhika have faced several hindrances in education. Her father was in Army force. In the time of armed conflict, her father was threatened to leave the job and joins the CPN (Maoist) party. But he denied doing so. And this denial became the cause of his death. He was killed when he was going to his office after the completion of vacation. After her father's death, her family was in painful situation. No one was there to help them and Radhika was the one who had to look after them. She had got the opportunity to go to school and study before the death of her father. But after the death of her father, she could not give enough time to education and was not mentally prepared to continue her education. Her time was invested in asking for justice to her family and also in consoling other family members. So the school going age was used for the household activities.

## A Bird-Eye View on Outcome of Interviews

From the study, it can be concluded that the school going children are becoming affected from both the state and the CPN (Maoist). The school going children were arrested by the state security forces for supporting the underground CPN (Maoist) rebels during the conflict and their family involvement in CPN (Maoist) party. CPN (Maoist) party also recruited those school going children by showing their surrounding social exclusion and poverty. Similarly, the CPN

(Maoist) party also killed the parents of the children for not giving money, and not supporting them or having different political ideologies. It shows that the school going age are compelled to hold a gun instead of a pen because of various reasons. Also they are compelled to do some income generating activities, household activities to support the family in the absence of the main person of the family. And some of them are still seeking the justice of their parents. It clearly shows that the child rights treaties, conventions are just in the document not in the practical life of the children in the era of ten years armed conflict. So it is the responsibility of all the stakeholders to provide affected friendly system of justice in order to ensure an efficient restoration and re-integration those conflict affected children into the society.

## Summary of the Chapter

I presented four cases of Sarada, Mahadev, Khim Bahadur and Radhika to delve how the school children experienced regarding their education during the ten years armed conflict. Due to poverty and over that being a Dalit, Sarada had faced social exclusion in society and school, she was motivated by the CPN (Maoist) political agendas and had left the school to join in the CPN (Maoist) revolution. Mahadev had lost his father as accepting different political ideology which was different from the CPN (Maoist) political ideology. He became an orphan and was bound to do labor as a breadwinner of his family. Similarly, Khim Bahadur had left school and joined the CPN (Maoist) cadre as the state security forces regularly tortured his family. So, he was compelled to join the CPN (Maoist) revolution rather than accepting the torture. And Radhika was affected as being the daughter of the state security personnel. When CPN (Maoist) killed her father, she was forced to leave school and imposed to work for family's survival as a senior family member. It clearly signifies that the involvement of parents in different political ideologies is the driving factor for the children being out of the reach of education. After the death of breadwinner, it had been a heavy burden on families and especially on children, who were school going children. So, it can be said that neither the state nor the CPN (Maoist) party was seen responsible to protect children's rights. As a result, children were deprived from the rights of education during the ten years armed conflict.

# 5

# Children's Experiences About their Life and Survival After the Peace Agreement as Panacea to Armed Conflict

## Things/Facts in the Womb

This chapter presents the analysis of data gathered through interview with the research participants. This chapter highlights the survival and the education of the conflict affected children at present. For the data collection, (i) in-depth interview was conducted. (ii) The information provided by the participants was recorded and (iii) themes were generated based on the interview.

## Facts and Hered to

The data gathered in the interview were kept without making any changes. Also the collected data were transcribed and interpreted in a meaningful way so that the meanings were not changed. The beginning of the chapter starts from the participants sharing about their experiences after the peace agreement. Furthermore, it includes (i) how they were behaved in the society, (ii) family's academic support, (iii)their educational status and students survival in the society Then, I have summarized my understandings in and then drew the a conclusion based on these data presented and thoroughly interpreted.

## After the Peace Agreement: Retirement and Justice

On 8 December 2006, the then Seven-Party Alliance Government and the CPN -Maoist signed the Agreement on the Monitoring of the Management of Arms and Armies (AMMAA), with the UN as witness, (ICG, 2011). The AMMAA sets out the words of the Nepal Army and the CPN (Maoist) army to support in building a free and fair atmosphere for the CA election. Similarly as per the provision 4.1.3 of the AMMAA - only those CPN (Maoist) Army Combatants who have been properly registered at cantonments will be qualified for possible integration into the security forces fulfilling the standard norms. Also under the AMMAA between the GoN, and the CPN (Maoist), it was agreed that the disqualified combatants should be immediately discharged from the cantonments. And it both parties are also committed to provide a choice between an economic package and various other alternatives for rehabilitation for ex-combatants.

## Commitments by Both Parties

So, after the CPA, both parties have committed to provide relief packages to those conflicts affected as per their need. As mentioned in the CPA, there were different relief packages for the conflict affected to address their problems and reintegrate them in the society (GoN, 2012). As per the rule, there were three provisions to choose for the CPN (Maoist) combatants: (i) reintegration into the Nepal army after going through the selection process under the mentioned standard set by the special committee, (ii) voluntary retirement of the combatants with golden handshake package that entailed the cash payment at the time of retirement and (iii) rehabilitation option with skill related training and seed money for them (ICG, 2011).

## Restrictions on Maoist Combatants

Based on the peace accord, Sarada was verified as a regular combatant by the UNMIN. After being verified as the CPN (Maoist) combatants in 2011, she could enter the selection round. However, she couldn't join the Nepal army because she did not have adequate education and also was only one child to take care of old parents, so she was compelled to leave the PLA with the option of self- retirement along with ten lakhs. She said that:

## Participants Response: Self-Retirement

After getting the information about the provision for PLA to integrate in the Nepal army, I was totally disappointed because there were certain limitations which needed to be addressed, like need to pass examination, physically able etc. But I had not adequate education and was not physically fit as injured in cross fighting in Lamjung, I could not integrated into the public system. So I thought I could not pass the criteria and decided to take self-retirement and return back to home. (Field note, 23 February 2015)

That means, she opted for the third option as rehabilitation opens with skill related training and provides seed money for them. And she returned to her own village. In this way, she came back to her own village by leaving the fighter's life.

## Response of Second Participant: Piteous and Painful

Khim has the similar case that Sarada had. According to the agreement between the government and the CPN (Maoist) party, PLA members had to stay in temporary cantonment till verification process. Khim said that, "as per the agreement and the provision of CPA, as a member of PLA, I had lived in the United Nations monitored cantonment waiting for the verification". He remembers his past as, "I spent five years in the cantonment but it was very difficult for me to meet my mother, when I met her she often used to cry by catching my hands". This situation was one of the reasons why he used to feel like getting out of the cantonment. After his five years stay in the cantonment, he was verified as a combatant by UNMIN which came to Nepal upon request of the GoN and the CPN (Maoist), as a special mission to support the peace agreement and to create a free and fair atmosphere for the election of the Constitutional Assembly (Upreti, 2009). Again, Khim said that:

## Averment of Participant

I was provided three options to choose as a combatant, I was interested to choose first option (integrate in Nepalese army), but my home environment, especially alone mother and my health could not give support as I was injured and was not fit for it, so I was enforced to choose third option (self-retirement). (Field note, 26 March 2015)

With this decision, he was partly happy and partly sad. He was happy because he could live with his mother and was sad as he could not fulfill his internal desire to serve the nation by being an army. He had taken the voluntary retirement of the combatants with golden handshake package program. And he received compensation of six lakhs to restart his lives.

## Voluntary Retirement and Return to Home

He said, "I went back to my home with the money and the wounds too. But this time I left the cantonment where I would not return again where he felt himself helpless". In a further query, he added that, "I have lost my father, my old mother is surviving alone remembering her disappeared son and dead husband, which really made my tears fall down".

## Participants Affection for his Family

While saying this, his gloomy face clearly reflected the pain within him. So to value the tears of his mother and to provide justice to the soul of his father, he registered the cases of his father who was killed by state security force and brother who got disappeared while Khim was underground. He shared, "at first the people denied to register the case saying that it was the political case and would be solved after the formation of TRC". This was the real situation that conflict affected faced. Again he added, "It has been a long time that I have returned from the cantonment and registered the case but still I am not getting any justice".

## Programmes of Development Organization: Only an Eye Wash

For the justice, "many development organizations as well as political parties have given words to search the disappeared members but it was just for the sake of search", said Khim. Still he was searching for help and justice, there were no ways ahead, similarly the case of disappearance people's situation is still unknown and their family could not get any information about their missing family member still now (OHCHR, 2012), whatever the authorized bodies give the commitment and word to find missing person. None of the cases had been solved and the disappeared brother was still missing. This really made me think that how the situation of the conflict affected is. So his life after the peace agreement is spent for the justice of his family members.

## Participant: A Little Bit Different Response

Different from the case of Sarada and Khim, Mahadev is struggling for the existence in his life after the peace agreement. After the peace agreement, he was happy knowing that all the criminals of the conflict would be punished and the adequate subsidy would be provided to the affected as mentioned in opted various commitment (OHCHR, 2012). He said that, "when I knew that the criminals would be punished, I shared it to my small brothers and sisters, and they became more than happy, my mother started to cry, maybe she had felt that her husband's soul would get peace". He again added that, "his mother asked him twice saying, would it come true? And would the criminals be punished?" This incident overwhelmed him and he convinced his mother by saying that he would register the case for the justice of his father.

## Actions Taken to Get Justice in Father's Case

Finally, Mahadev registered the case. He tried to find the truth but couldn't get it because of political instability. Also he said that he had no one to talk for the case so he couldn't get justice.

## Threats and Suppression Started

He had tried to get justice but he was threatened by the CPN (Maoist) people not to register the case and for the withdrawal after registration. He said that one of the CPN (Maoist) cadres has threatened him by saying, "your father used to say about ours to the police personnel so he was killed. It would be better to withdraw the case as we have several similar cases that were killed and disappeared due to your father. So you must do as per we say otherwise you have to think about your life". In this way he was getting more trouble after the peace agreement which was beyond his thinking.

## Case of Muder and Disappearance Withdrawn

Similarly the study of Advocacy Forum and Human Rights Watch (2011) highlighted that there are many case of murder and disappearance which are withdraw* without any investigation by both side. As a result, the suffered families were becoming more burn. It happened due to the lack of proper utilization of TRC with the different political interest of the leaders. He used to think that the affected are getting more mental torture in this time and are not getting the justice. In this way, he is passing his time after the peace agreement.

## Troubles of Fourth Participant Radhika

Radhika, who was having a similar case like that of Mahadev was also being affected for being a daughter of the state security personnel and is still not getting help from the state. In query about the peace agreement, she said that, "at first I was unknown about the peace agreement as I was always busy in doing my household activities." One of her maternal uncle shared with her about the provision after the peace agreement to the armed conflict affected family. Only then she started to search the truth and justice. She had visited several chief army personnel but could not get any information justice about the death of her father. For this she had also visited Karnel Thapa (pseudonym), army personnel who were the true friends of her father, for the justice but he responded it as, "it's a political case and what the government does it matters.

## Friends Turned Foes

We can't do anything except providing sympathy. Wait for some time, TRC will help you to get justice." After meeting Thapa, she returned to her home with the empty hands where her mother was expecting some great achievement. She said, "I was unable to fulfill my mother's expectations, I thought, if I were the son of my father I would get help. Because of being daughter, I was not helped by anybody." She felt inferior on her own. In a disappointing voice she said that, "TRC is formed after long time of the CPA and the implementation was weak so the affected like me were not getting justice and I don't think they would ever get justice." So she said that it's like a poem "aama tyo aauchhara" (mother, will it come)? Where mother says it will come in the future. Similarly, all the people around her used to say that they will get justice in the future but future is like the poem. She is also passing time in doing the household activities and with the little hope of getting justice.

## Only False Condolence for Missing Person and those Murdered

The hope of the affected is still alive for getting the justice for the dead and disappeared, but neither GoN nor CPN (M) take the ownership of accident and provide the justice (Human Rights Watch &Advocacy Forum, 2011).

From the four participants of the study, I concluded that none of them were getting adequate justice which they intended to get. Neither the government nor the CPN (Maoist) party was providing justice. So the affected were being more affected day by day even after the peace agreement.

## Reintegration in the Society

Reintegration in the society is the survival technique of the conflict affected children's after the peace agreement while having to face several challenges ahead.

## Social Exclusion and Discri* Persists

After returning the village, Sarada could not get good environment as she has thought. She explains, "I was not accepted in the society as some of the neighbors said that I came back by killing several people and was sinful". By remembering this she again felt unpleasant and recalled, "It was my compulsion to hold a gun and fight against the social system for the justice and freedom but now I am not accepted". This shows the sorrows and sympathy of being involved in CPN (Maoist) party.

## Humiliation, ill Treatment in Society

Likewise, according to Sarada, "the neighbors are still afraid of her and don't talk with her" which is also included in the report of Partnerships for Protecting Children in Armed Conflict (2010).

In many cases, she was excluded and was not informed in several programs and social welfare activities. She shared about the event what she faced, "One day when I went to a *puja* organized by my uncle, where my neighbors and relatives were also invited, I was excluded by some female of the society". They said that, "we can't give the entry to do puja of our religion for the Sarada who is sinful by killing people". In a weeping sound she further said that, "my uncle and aunt tried to convince to the people but they are also against the aunt and uncle and they are ready to leave the *puja* if they include me in the puja." By this incident she was compelled to leave the puja and attend other social and religious programs. Women and girls face problems returning to normality after war's end due to value systems based upon honor and shame (Afshar & Eade, 2004) which has made Sarada felt inferior.

## Different Type of Discrimination in Society

She tried herself to participate in several programs like different marital functions, pujas, festivals but it was not an easy way to get easy reintegration in the society. Once, she requested a training center to provide training on tailoring. At first they denied, but with several request, they agreed to provide training. On the first day of the training, she was returning to her home with her friends, she listened that *Arati* (pseudonym) was planning to have some snacks on the way but *Rita* (pseudonym) refused saying, "what will the society say on having snacks with Sarada?" This made her either to continue the training or to leave it. With the dilemmas, she continued it. She even joined the tailoring course for her livelihood but other participants left the course because of her participation. It is similar situation with Indian conflicts affected women there is colossal discrimination with conflict affected women in society and nobody trusts them (Qayoom, 2014).

## No Use of Peace Treaty

She was interested to do some skill related works for her livelihood. But the situation was not favorable. She didn't get any place to even open the tailoring shop. She added, "In this world no one is helpful and one has to manage oneself so I have no education and have to manage myself to do some work for livelihood and to sustain."

## Social Discrimination in Vogue

Similarly the study of Partnerships for Protecting Children in Armed Conflict (2010) also finds that returning girls and young women from the armed conflict in particular face some discrimination due to cultural norms and hard accepted in their society. As a PLA member, Sarada has experienced some discrimination on return to her communities.

## Credibility and Confidence Gone: Poor Women

Similarly, she wanted to invest the amount that was provided through relief program in the partnership business but she could not do that because no one believed her. They used to say that, "we cannot do partnership with you because we still are afraid with the works that you did." For investing alone she needed some extra money and she had asked with the neighbors and relatives but they did not help her. When she had asked for money with her relatives, they said that, "you must have money when you have captured those banks, so why you need money from us? Capturing bank is insufficient?" When she begged with another person, he said that, "you are coming just to show that you don't have money. Where have you kept the money that you have captured in the conflict time? Are you digging and keeping the money?" This directly reflects how the conflicts affected were struggling for reintegration.

## Fair Deeds Receiving Humiliation

Likewise, the report of Partnerships for Protecting Children in Armed Conflict (2010) focused on the conflict affected especially girls and women and stated that they were facing difficulties to adjust in their society in Nepal with the behaviors of other people in society.

## Shower of Blames and Allegations

Sarada also felt same as the report of PPCAC, she felt a kind of shame; she was more discriminated than she was in the society before joining the CPN (Maoist) movement. She had no more options and was in dilemma about what to do.

## Piteous Condition of those not Joined CPN (Maoist)

Mahadev felt helpless, for not being a CPN (Maoist). He was surrounded by the neighbors who were CPN (Maoist) and had fought in the armed conflict against the government. He neither could leave that place nor live in the existing home. The leaders of the CPN (Maoist) party and other neighbors tended to make him a CPN (Maoist) otherwise they would blame and would say that he was not social for not being a CPN (Maoist) and he was not getting help too. He remembers, "when I had loan from a cooperative for buying goats and buffalos for my home, the members of the cooperative were all my neighbors and they denied to help me" by saying that, "You are not a CPN (Maoist) and also you can't pay the loan back as your father is already dead and you do not have any income generating sources."

## Political Bias from People

He further said that he could see political bias from people around him. And all the social aspects are taken politically as he has different political ideology. He added that, "Such incidents always recall the memories of my father, if he was alive, we would not get such difficulties for the reintegration in the society." He said that, "For asking help for my livelihood nobody helped me so the government should support the affected children like me." In this regards, IHRC (2013) also states that that government should provide loan and should invest for business purpose so that the affected like him could sustain easily in the society and it would be the respect for the killed ones.

## Neighbor Became Rival/Foe

He expressed a bitter truth on what the neighbors said in this regards. He shared that the people didn't believe that as he had no one to help and he had lost his father so how he could pay the money back. He felt helpless and he was suffering from the pity situation. In one side, he had the pain of losing his father and not getting justice, and on the other hand, he have to take care of his family and not getting any help. So he felt it like, "*baleko aagoma gheeu thane kaam*" (adding ghee/butter in the burning fire) with the behavior that the people were doing. The society has always seen the conflict affected in different ways as they were the reasons for the unsocial environment (PPCAC, 2010). This is clearly seen in the Khim's daily life.

## Peace has Piercing Experience

Khim, with the thinking of changing the society, faced several hindrances in the society for the social acceptance. He has the similar case as of Sarada. He is totally ignored by the society. When his mother was ill then nobody took a good care of her. He remembered, "It was Ashad, 27, I was in the farm for planting rice, my mother was alone at home, and she faced a severe headache and fever and asked her neighbor to help her by providing a glass of hot water but she was neglected." He further adds, "When I came back to my home from work, she was sleeping in an unconscious condition because of fever, so I carried her on my back to hospital. After her consciousness, she shared the case of the aunt who did not help." He felt sadness about his mother who was alone the whole day. Also, some of the neighbors were even saying that, "She is witch and because of her, she has lost her husband, family members are also not happy, daughter in law ran away and son was in the war." This situation really made him very sad.

Similarly, when his mother was ill next month, and he asked his friend who was his schoolmate to take her to hospital, he did not help him. He remembered that his friends even said that:

## Scars of Being CPN (Maoist) Member

I am unable to help your mother as you are the members of the CPN (Maoist) group, and if I help you, the police will arrest me. Can't you remember, when I have helped your mother when you were underground, the police have arrested me and kept me in jail for 2 months? (Field note, 26 March 2015)

This really made Khim very sad. He was in a dim face when he was sharing this. Keeping a hand in his head and showing the pictures of his school days, he said that he requested another friend in the picture, he too didn't help him. He faced several social discriminations in the society (PPCAC, 2010). He said that instead of being supportive, his society and neighbor always played a negative role. He was happy neither with the state nor with the CPN (Maoist) party for not getting any kind of social support for reintegration.

## Conflict Affected Women: Facing Atrocities

Radhika, being affected from the CPN (Maoist) political parties could not adjust in the society. She was socially, culturally, facing different discrimination. Though armed conflict sometimes facilitates changes in traditional gender relations (Afshar & Eade, 2004), it is not seen in the case of Radhika. Also she was facing several gender discriminations. One day when she was in the water tap to carry water, Sita (pseudonym) asked if she had got some help as conflict affected, she said she had not. Then Sita replied; "If you were the son then you could do some work for the livelihood of the family but being a daughter your role is only carrying water and doing household activities. So your family is facing pitiable situation because of extreme poverty and not getting help as conflict affected."

## Living Unmarried is also Painful

She felt pity on herself for being unmarried as the society blames her in different ways. Once when a Lieutenant General was there for the discussion to marry with Radhika, one of the neighbors had said that she was not good in the society as she had lost her father and nobody was there to take care of her. The marriage was cancelled at the last minute. This incident really made her more serious of being alive in the society. She couldn't speak sometime and started to cry remembering those incidents. Later on, after drinking a glass of water, she shared that, "I should also have been killed when the people have killed my father. Death is better than living and facing several hindrances in the society."

## Relatives Turned Looters/Plunders

She said that, "There are several challenges and hindrances ahead of me. Even my uncle has taken some land which is fertile." She shared the incidents with some educated people of the society about the issue of land but they said that it was their family matter and they had nothing to do with it. Interference of the people of the society is not good in the family matter. In this aspect, being a female in the society, she faced several challenges in the society. Neither did she get adequate help and support from the government side, nor did the people in the society and her relatives or she do anything alone to fight against the social and gender discrimination, and domination. Asian Human Rights Commission study (2013) also agreed that especially women and girl faced several challenges and hindrances conflict in post conflict situation. Neither their relatives helped them nor could people of community not have helped them after the death of father. So, they become more affected and marginalized.

In this way, the conflict affected children were facing several challenges and problems in the reintegration within the society even after the peace agreement. The interview showed that how miserable the situation of conflict affected children was.

## Education After the Peace Agreement

In this part, the need of education and the interest of the conflict affected children in continuing their education have been explored. Also the barriers and challenges they faced in regards to getting education after the peace agreement have been highlighted.

## Age Gap: A Strong Barrier

Sarada had several challenges and problems to be solved so the educational need has not been the priority for her. In a query about the education that she wanted to join, she said that "My school friends are educated and settled but I am still struggling for the basic needs." She added that, "If I even continue the study, the age gap between me and other children doesn't help me to go to school and continue my study, so how could I study with the small children in the same class?" It was almost 16 years ago that she left school education and it would be difficult to read and write again being a secondary level student. She further added that, "My brain could not catch the knowledge shared in the school so it would not be possible to join the school again." Some of the children of her friends are in the same school and it would be odd for her to be their classmate. When she had money to spend, she did not have anyone to invest in their education. She had tears in her eyes while saying this and she remembered her sister saying, "If my sister was alive then I would have invested the money that was provided in self-retirement on her education, but I don't have anyone." Education was beyond her thinking. And the provided money was also almost finished by fulfilling the basic needs, so she had other major issues to solve rather than getting education.

## Overage Issue: Another Barrier

Mahadev was one of the affected who had courage and enthusiasm to continue his study. But because of age limitation (18 years) which is determined in the provision in CPA, he was over 18 years and couldn't get help from the government for his study. He got some support from organizations that helped him to continue his study. He said, "I did private SLC with the help of the school teacher who was also a friend of my father." He had deep interest to study further but he couldn't do it. He added, "I have a kin interest to continue my education but don't have enough money so, I started working in the school as a primary level teacher." Again he added, "The money was not good enough for the livelihood. In this situation, how could I continue my study by paying fee to the colleges? I couldn't do my 10+2 if the development organization hadn't helped me." But it was very difficult for him to go to the collage and study as his friends were small brothers and sisters of his society. His brother and sister were also provided scholarship so there was some relief to Mahadev. Recently, he was doing the private B.Ed. but the organization was not helping him as it was only focused for the 10+2 education. Besides, he was teaching in a private school which was only the means to sustain.

## Overage: A Curse on Way to Acquire Education

His mother was always worried about her children's study and job. So he sent his brother and sister to college though he had several difficulties to pay the fees. Shanti Samiti had also provided his brothers and sisters (who were under the age of 18) with some scholarship for intermediate level. The statement, "But who is responsible for educating my brothers and sisters when they get above the age of 18?" was one of the pertinent issues raised by Mahadev. The scholarship was not adequate and it was Mahadev to provide the money for the school uniform, reading and other materials for his brothers and sisters. So he was more focused on the education of his brothers and sisters. Though the CPA focused on the help and support for the conflict affected, he disagreed on it. He shared:

## Guarantee for Future: Paramount Need

We, conflict affected don't want short term help but guarantee for our future is needed. The basic needs need to be fulfilled. For me, if the pension of my father is provided, it would help me to spend on my brothers' and sisters' education and I will also save it for their future so that I can save my salary for my education. (Field note, 3 March 2015)

## Assistance Expected to Continue Education

From the sayings, Mahadev was one of the conflicts affected who wanted to study further. He was also seeking some help and support to continue his study. He had several compulsions but also he was continuing his study and sending his small brothers and sisters to schools. In a different context, he asked why the festivals come to make the poor more poor as he could not fulfill the demands of the family. He becomes sadder when the New Year comes as it is for the new session of the brothers and sisters where he has to spend extra money for the admission and learning materials. He wanted to study in a good environment but he couldn't do so as he had to take care of the family members.

## Responsibilities First – Education Next

Khim, third participant of the study, did not want to continue his education. He was the main person of the family so he had several responsibilities to fulfill. He said, "I am too old to join the school and continue the study. It's time to do something for the livelihood so I don't want to continue my study." With a slight smile, he added, "how to join school and study with the children as classmates." This issue was not because of only the social restrictions but the age bar was also major. Being an adult, he did not want to join the school; rather he needed some help to make a living.

Radhika, coming back from the suffering of her father's death to normal life, did not want to continue her study. She emphasized that she did not want to rejoin formal education. She added, "I have several responsibilities to perform in the family, and also I do not have the amount of money that I need to spend in my education." She has responsibility to make assimilation and accommodation of her family.

## Problem of Catering to Family Needs

She added: "My old grandfather and grandmother are suffering from different old age pains, psychological problems, worries and I even was not able to provide a cetamol *(medicinal tablet for fever)*, in this situation how could I think about education of my own?" (Field note, 17 April 2015).

## Some other Issues

Her mother was suffering from mental disease after the death of her husband, and she was not able to provide counseling treatment with doctors which was the major concern and priority for her. So she had faced very aching situation and education was in the shadow. She was suffering from different hindrances and barriers for her livelihood. She said that the society was talking about her and her family in negative way. She added:

## Responsibility to Look After Family

It has been already the age that I have to marry but I couldn't leave my family in this situation. I have the responsibility to take care of my family after my father's death. So government should provide some incentives and income generating activities. Still all the affected are not getting adequate compensation. If I look around me, my brothers and sisters are not getting adequate scholarship. The scholarship is limited within 10+2 level students who are under the age of 18. The amount is only Rs.16000 per year. So scholarship for the conflict affected in higher education should be increased and all the affected should get free education until they are interested and job should be made secured for those affected. (Field note, 17 April 2015)

## Need for Sustainable Livelihood

From her sayings, it was clear that the conflict affected need a sustainable livelihood of their family. Education was not a matter. So she was more focused on education of her small brothers and sisters, taking care of her mother and grandmother. She wondered if the government could provide some loans and scholarship for the conflict affected like her, she couldn't take more burdens on the education of other family members.

## Livelihood Security

This part is about the support provided to the participants after the peace agreement. Furthermore, it focuses on what support the conflict affected children have got in the post conflict situation.

## Pain of People who Got Voluntary Retirement

Sarada, who used to say that she was fighting for the nation had to get self-retirement from the PLA. With this, she got 6 lakhs in installment by the government as stated in the CPA. She said that, "Only the amount of six lakhs has not supported me or my family to fulfill the basic needs, so in this situation, how could I be happy?" She also added, "The loss of the family members can't be compensated by the money." Her voices clearly showed that she was still facing the absence of her father. So she said, "Before the armed conflict we were happy within the poverty and social discrimination but now by getting some money also we cannot be happy." In a query of who had helped them apart from the government, she added, "Many organizations working in the issues of conflict affected came to me and showed the hope that they would provide other help but I could not get any other help." From this also, it was clear that the development partners were not providing the support to the real affected.

## Distribution of Money Illicit Ways

Sarada told that she had fought for the liberation of the country but with increasing awareness level of the people there were no such changes. The society is the same, corruption has increased. She added that the money provided for the affected of the armed conflict might have been distributed to other people who were not the real affected so she hadn't got money and any facilities. She further said that:

> I have listened that several funds are provided to different INGOs, NGOs, DDC, VDC for the relief program to the affected but I haven't got a single rupee. I used to see several news coverage about these types of programs in the radio, television, newspaper. No one is helping us. We worked for the nation's good, people's help but proper respect and programs are not implemented for the conflict affected and their families. (Field note, 23 February 2015)

## What Does Media Say?

Her sayings were similar with the report of International Human Rights Clinic (2013). It stated that there was misusage of huge amount of money and the target groups were not getting the benefits. She has got a proof that a neighbor received the beautician training in the name of conflict affected who was not exactly the conflict affected. She said that, "My neighbor was there because she had some links with other political leaders who had referred to her, so the real affected were not getting the exact relief programs." Therefore, the real affected were facing several problems as the fake affected were using power and getting relief materials in the name of the affected people.

Mahadev blamed himself for not being the people of either CPN (Maoist) or the government. So the help was not provided what he had to get. He added that:

## Regret on Not Joining any Groups

My father was the school teacher so none of the sides takes care of him. If he was the member of any political party then we would be provided some help and support like others and they would even respect my father but we do not have any links with the high level leaders of any political parties and why would they help us? (Field note, 3 March, 2015)

This disagreement and the reality of Mahadev made us think again about the political discrimination in the society that still existed within the power holders. The affected who had some linkage with the political parties were getting help and support but who did not have they were not getting such help that the affected were supposed to get. He questioned, "Will 1 lakh as per the interim relief program in installment through the government fulfill the absence of my father?" He further shared, "It was just like the showing teeth of the elephant which have neither the value nor the beauty." And the relief programs were only limited to the people who had power and politics. Again he added that:

I have listened that some amount of money was allocated for the conflict affected from an organization (did not want to disclose the name) but it was taken by the humanitarian society for doing some works but still the works are not done and the people didn't return back. (Field note, 3 March 2015)

## "Might is Right" Dictum Prevails

It also showed that the affected were more affected by the people who had power. So he said that the conflicts affected were being the media for getting money by the powerful people in the name of the conflict people.

## Age stand as bar for Scholarships

He got limited scholarship programs to his small brothers and sisters but he could not get it as he was already above 18 years. He got some help from development organizations for his study as the family of the killed people in the conflict. The school fees were given but it was very limited and was not enough. He added that, "It was not enough but it helped me in some way." So to get the relief program, he added that:

### Ask Support of Powerful People

I should be the powerful person or the relatives of powerful persons to get the help from the organizations. Whoever have the power they get help in an easy way, but the affected people like me who do not have power don't get help. (Field note, 3 March 2015)

Similarly, Khim was another affected of the conflict who was still struggling for the relief programs. He got 6 lakhs in installment from the government for self-retirement from PLA. He told:

### Relief not Provided

I have heard that the government should provide treatment to the affected like me who were physically and psychologically traumatized, such as free medical care and other reparation to the families of those who are killed in armed conflict but it was not provided adequately to me and my family. (Field note, 26 March, 2015)

According to Khim's interview, it was known that the government had provided limited support as compensation without analyzing the circumstances of the affected. He said, "I have got Rs 50,000 as I have ¼ disabilities as ascertained in percentage term for my treatment but is not sufficient to fully recover to my disabilities".

### Contention

He suggested, "According to the nature of the trauma of the affected, the government must provide adequate support for me." His saying showed that he was physically weak and needed some help for the treatment. He was waiting for more financial and other support for his recuperation. In this regards, he said:

### Table of Frail and Lean Body Person

I have problem in my arm after being beaten by the armies. The incident has already happened to me, and I'm not going to get it back. I have stomach problems and swelling also. I am unable to go to the hospital for my treatment because of poverty. Our families still suffer from psychological and physical tolerance of armed conflict. I and my family become the often-overlooked affected of the ongoing strife, our plight exacerbated by poverty and abuse. So I need both legal and economic support more than education support. (Field note, 3 March, 2015)

## Support or Relief Falls Short of Need

And as affected of the armed conflict, he said, "I had received the support and that support has proved inadequate for affected like me; it's like providing a doll to kid to make him or her forget sad experience for some moment." It shows that the government was not fully responsible in case of the injured. And some of the injured were still not getting the relief packages (National Institute for Policy Studies [NIPS], 2013). Consequently, he added, the government reimbursed bills for treatment costs, but it did not reimburse treatment in private hospitals and it was not possible for all those conflict affected to take the treatment through government hospital because of inadequate government hospitals in Nepal.

Similarly, the affected could not receive any financial allowance for treatment for full recovery (Devkota, 2014), and he received no financial assistance for the follow-up treatment. He added with a heartrending voice that:

## Claim for Relief

I have borrowed money for treatment and medicine, and will have to pay next year. I am now physically not able to work. The injury during the conflict time has really made me difficult to work and survive. Everything has been difficult and complex in my life today. (Field note, 3 March 2015)

## Relief Must Cure – Irritation & Anxiety

It can be said that he had been suffering greatly from feelings of irritation and anxiety about day-to-day life, problems with self-care, discussions with other members of the family, crisis in thinking about the future, and confusion over everyday decisions. And still he was unable to pay the debt. So the people who helped him were always torturing him by continuously saying him to pay the money back but he had no any option. So he added, "I do not have any option to ask the money for my follow up and treatment to those people who have already helped me and I am unable to pay the debt." He requested, "The government should be more responsible to fulfill such needs of the affected."

## Apathy by Leaders and Bureaucratic

And he complained that the "interim relief" system was not affected centric. The impractical implementation procedures compounded by bureaucratic apathy and politicized (NIPS, 2013) made him more frustrated. He complained, "The system of interim relief is generally insensitive towards the affected." The numbers of categories of affected were left out altogether; those that were entitled to relief also faced problems in accessing it due to a number of reasons. It seemed that the need analysis was the only way to fulfill the needs of the affected.

## Lack of Effective Help from Government

Radhika said that ten years had passed after the Nepal's armed conflict; but still civilian affected are struggling in the absence of effective help from the government. She said that, "I had got 10 lakhs as a relief program from the state in installment basis for the death of my father". She added:

My neighboring uncle collected the economic assistance provided by the government to the family of the conflict affected. But I didn't know much about the assistance offered and money cannot compensate the loss of my father. He lost his life being patriotic. (Field note, 17 April, 2015)

### Relatives Gobbled Relief Fund

She said, "I am little aware about the relief programs that is provided by the state and different organizations. My uncle is the one who knows everything and he takes some relief materials which are provided in our name." She had heard that different organizations were providing different skill based trainings but she was unable to go there as she had to take care of her mother and grandmother. She even did not know some programs that were held in the society for the conflict affected.

### Interim Relief Package: Only Eye Wash

She criticized the government's minor support to the conflict affected through interim relief packages. She added, "Without the needs, aspirations and demands of affected, the government has distributed the support programs to show the sympathy towards us, and I don't think it would be long lasting." None of the relief providers ever visited to her. Her uncle have taken all the details and she was even not given the information. She told that many of fake conflict affected received relief packages although some real affected were denied because of lacking political power. She said:

### Fake Documents and Political Influence Main Recipients of Relief

Local leaders who are not conflict affected have been getting compensation and relief packages by submitting fake documents and exercising political influence. In this situation, how could we believe that the TRC, with its members picked by the political parties, will not be biased? (Field note, 17 April, 2015)

## Ineligible Welcomed-Eligible Ousted

She blamed that people close to the political leaders had received the package funds even though their level of affected did not reach the established criteria for receiving it. So it can be said that whatever these relief programs had been implemented, there were inconsistencies and allegations of exclusion. Hence, the implementation of these packages did not lack controversy and criticism. Moreover, the real conflict affected family received neither justice nor adequate reparations, though it has been years since the conflict ended. It is also supported by IHRC (2013) as "government relief program, set to end in 2014, has failed to deliver sufficient services and support to the family of the affected." The report also highlighted that the relief programs were not affected centered so they had not been implemented properly.

## Gross Ignorance Shown by State

Through the interview with her, she was found to be very frustrated with the transitional justice process. She said, "The state was completely ignoring the affected demands." She also felt, "The professional human rights activists were not paying attention to their key needs and demands, but rather sought to 'Instrumentalized' conflict affected for their own ends." She realized that it was necessary for all affected to come together to forge a common position and voice to create pressure to the government.

## Present Situation and Need

This present situation is the situation of the conflict affected children after the peace agreement. This indicates how they are living in the present situation and what their present needs are.

## Was it My Sin to Involve in War?

From the interview with Sarada, it could be said that, the present situation of the conflict affected is still miserable. She said, "I neither got great respect so I could be proud of joining the CPN (Maoist) movement nor I became happy with the traditional thinking of the people of the society for what I joined the CPN (Maoist) movement." This shows that the self-retirement has not been good for her. She is facing several hindrances and feeling isolated in the society. No one is ready to help her. She is feeling helpless and no one is guiding her and her family. She said that:

> Living in this isolated society as a *ladaku* (fighters) is very painful; it would be more fruitful if I had lost my life in the war, I shouldn't see these types of circumstances in the society. I was fighting for the people's freedom but now I myself am feeling the exclusions from the people. (Field note, 23 February 2015)

She further questioned, "Is it my sin to be involved in the war?" This clearly showed that how miserable the situation of the conflict affected was. They are not getting any kind of opportunity. The only way for Sarada is to wait and see what will happen in the future. Not only this, but she is facing other challenges ahead for the sustainable livelihood. She said that:

## Education Proved by Government to Needs

One of the most challenging things is that my education doesn't help me to join in good posts in the offices; even it was not the adequate qualification to do official works as I had left the school in the early classes. (Field note, 23 February 2015)

This showed that the affected like her who left school education in the early time are facing academic challenges to get the job now.

She further added, "Joining the school again is not the area of my interest as other aspects like taking care of the family, maintaining the household needs are major and compulsion for me."

The crucial aspect of the interview was that she wanted to do some work for her livelihood. She added:

### Work Need for Livelihood

Only relying on the money provided from the relief program couldn't become sustainable for me as I had old parents who need daily care and medicines, thus I am searching the work to fulfill the current needs of the family in this expensive market. (Field note, 23 February, 2015)

So having employment in some skill based task for the livelihood is the pertinent issue for her. Thus, her interest, ability and capability demand skill based works. For this she has requested to forward her voices to the responsible authority and for the effective monitoring of the ex-combatants issues which has not been done by the state (NIPS, 2013).

### Pain of Next Participant

Sarada became affected by her interest to get involved in the CPN (Maoist) movement but Mahadev was being affected for his father's cause. It is still unknown that who had exactly killed Mahadev's father. So he requested, "The punishment should be done to those people who were involved in killing my father." At present he is struggling to make money for his study. He said, "I couldn't get any kind of support from the people of the society, so I myself have to search money for my study." After the death of his father, he has become the breadwinner of the family. So he has no any options to think about himself. He added:

## How to Continue Education?

I have strong desire to continue my study but there are several challenges ahead. I have continued 10+2 education by the help of the organization, salary from my job. But now the organizations are not helping and I have to manage it myself. (Field note, 3 March 2015)

His strong desire to continue his education has made him successful to read at this level. And also he is contributing to the family along with his study. His main responsibility is not to give a chance to feel the absence of his father in his family. Time and again, the society has changed and the market price is also very high.

So, he shares, "Only my income is not sufficient to cover all the needs of the family." He added:

## Lack of High Qualification

In all the places and vacancies, there is a demand of highly qualified persons with experiences but I don't have that so it has been a great challenge for me to get good job that would help for the livelihood. So I wanted to continue my education. (Field note, 3 March, 2015)

## Government Sanction Loan

He said that he wanted to do some work but he did not have any money to invest. Even he did not have enough property to use. So he feels that government should provide loan without interest for the affected. "For the educated one, loans should be provided by keeping their certificates as the property", he added. He wanted to do something with the help from the government. In this regards, Farasa and Hayner (2009) stated that the government needs to introduce the affected centered program to address their needs, sustain their livelihood and make the success of peace agreement in Nepal.

## What Should Government Do?

As per the need of affected, government should introduced the program and provide them (NIPS, 2013). So, the government needs to listen to the voices of those conflict affected. Mahadev expressed:

### A Bunch of Necessities

I require different types of support like financial, social, and psychological to deal with these effects of the armed conflict. I need financial aid to meet the basic needs of my family. Looking to the future, I need job, training and employment opportunities, and educational support for me and my family. (Field note, 3 March 2015)

He recurrently identified non-material as well as material needs and expectations. He also mentioned that government should provide some long term programs for future life than merely providing short term programs which do not help them properly (NIPS, 2013).

### Distinct Problems Also Exist

Mahadev is struggling for his education and support for the family members but Khim Bahadur has a different situation. His brother is still disappearing, his sister in law has left his home and mother was living alone in the society. He has asked the government and the CPN (Maoist) party to search his brother, but, he added, "no one is doing it seriously and there is no any news about my brother". So he is still in search of the disappeared member of his family. He believed: "I can't do anything only by myself and the money provided by the government is not sufficient as I had to take care of my mother, small children of my brother and I don't have good qualification to search a good job" (Field note, 26 March 2015).

In a query about the continuation of his education, he laughed and said:

## Armed Conflict: Ousted Education

*Padhai ta sabai yuddha le lagyo,banduk le khayo* (Education is missed by getting involved in the armed conflict), leaving pen, carrying gun and again catching pen is not suitable for me as I have to take other responsibilities of my family, and also I don't have interest to continue my education. (Field note, 26 March 2015)

So, he is in a dilemma what to and what not to do. He has a very disappointing situation at his home. His mother always remembers his son who has been disappeared in the conflict era. And he also feels the same, "If my brother was there he could help me and I shouldn't take all the burden of the family." He still thinks that his brother is alive and will return home one day. He said:

## False Commitments of Leaders

It's been more than 10 years and we are still in search of our brother. During the war-time, we were told that the CPN (Maoist) party will look after us in case something would happen to our brother but the party leaders never came back. (Field note, 26 March 2015)

This was really a miserable situation for the families who are unknown about the situation of the disappeared family members (Shakya, 2006). Similarly there is incredible impact on families' member of those armed conflict affected as faced by Khim.

## Guilty to be Punished

He suggested that there should be some policies to punish the people who had done crime in the society as mentioned on CPA, if not then the crime would increase in the society, anyone can kill people and they can live carefree. He further added that the situation of the disappeared should be known as fast as possible and should punish the guilty that had done such work. He shared that he neither became able to provide punishment to those people nor was able to take care of his family when they were in the need of help. But he is happy about what he did against the social discrimination and crime.

### Problem of Unemployment

He added that it was very difficult for him to pass through the situation. He thought to go abroad after getting treatment. He further added, "Mother will be alone so I and my mother came to a conclusion that I should marry and go abroad so that my mother won't feel lonely." He disclosed no one was ready to get their daughter married with me as I don't have any job and was the CPN (Maoist) supporter. At that moment he thought that he was not a good son, good brother as he could not fulfill the necessity of his family. So this resulted in self -stigmatization in post conflict situation and become helpless (Pherali, 2011). Still he faced that, "even the shopkeepers are scared of me when I used to go there to take some food and necessary materials. This made me disgraceful on what I did in the past."

### Long Term Relief Programmes to be Launched

Khim further said, "The provided short term programs are not being so helpful for the affected, so long term programs should be run; new programs should be launched targeting the affected." He also stated that government and other donor agencies should think on the long term program that will help the conflict affected to sustain. Similarly, the commissions on truth and reconciliation and on investigation of the disappeared persons should be formulated and implemented properly (NIPS, 2013). It should be free from politicization to ensure the affected right to justice.

## Supreme Court Verdict: Neglected

Many children became orphan as their parents were killed by the CPN (Maoist) party who accused them for being security person like Radhika's father. She had searched and fought for justice of her father many years. After signing the Comprehensive Peace Accord, Radhika's families were very happy with the decision of Supreme Court. The decision of 1st June, 2007 was about finding the criminals who were involved in disappearing and killing people and punishing (Upreti, 2009), but none of the components of that decision have been implemented yet, said Radhika. She added, "I felt that this has made the criminals free." She further stated:

## Criminals Defended

Those responsible people of my father's death remain in the politics; Pitamber Pandey (pseudonym) is now leader of the CPN (Maoist) party. He denied detaining my father, and 17 years later the CPN (Maoist) party still doesn't formally accept that they had killed my father. (Field note, 17 April, 2015)

So she felt that the rights of the affected were not respected and because of this also they were not feeling good in the society. In this regard, she added:

## Criminals have Political Influence Gained

I and my family, the surviving families of the dead people, continue to live every day through the grief of not knowing the truth about our loved ones. We lost the main person of our family but no one is taking responsibility of this and the criminals are seen around. And we still face security threats from CPN (Maoist) party. The perpetrators of the disappearances and killings during the war are in positions of power and many have been promoted politically. So we became voiceless even we are in injustice. We have dream of justice and dignity, but first we want the truth of why and how our family members are killed. Our family life has been destroyed, ruined, many of us lost bread-winners, and our unmitigated grief has no closure. Who is responsible for this? What does 'family' mean, after all? Can the state and the politicians ever compensate for the loss of our family life? I want to question it with accused person and government. (Field note, 17 April, 2015)

She was in fear and angry while expressing her internal pain. Her sayings were very true on what she had felt in the society where she was not getting justice. It showed both parties have failed to materialize their promise to seek justice for affected of human rights violations including sexual violence, and to end impunity (Human Rights Watch, 2014).

## A Cluster of Misfortune

Also, it seemed that she was transforming the pain to strength and was ready to fight against the law. But she was facing problems to fulfill the basic needs of the family. She said:

> Even I can't provide small medical help to my mother and grandmother. Neither I had enough property nor do I have enough education to find a good job and I am doing all the works for my mother and grandmother's happiness. So I had no time to think about myself. (Field note, 17 April, 2015)

## Depression Does not Allow Continuing Education

This shows that she did not have mentality to study again rather she was focused on caring her mother and grandmother. After the death of her father, she has been facing severe poverty problem and she was also mentally depressed and no one was there to help her. She was struggling alone. After listening to the interview of Radhika, it could be deduced that the family members of the deceased want to know that perpetrators were held accountable, the affected were ensured justice, and denounced amnesty in those cases of massive human rights violations which happened in the armed conflict and taking a great responsibility in the small age for the fulfillment of the family's needs.

## Demands of Conflict Affected: Left Unheard

The expressions of Radhika intended to seek some help from the government but the demand of the conflict affected was not heard by the responsible authority. "There are several organizations working in the field of conflict affected and their education but the real affected are still searching help" said Radhika. She further added:

## Things Suggested in Public Welfare

Different trainings for the income generating programs like beautician, tailoring, goat farming, and agriculture should be focused for the people like me who couldn't go to school and work in offices as I don't have adequate academic qualification. So I need some effective programs that should be launched focusing us. (Field note, 17 April 2015)

Her saying regarding her interest for the sustainable livelihood showed that it was a better opportunity for the uneducated conflict affected. And she was not satisfied with government compensation. Only providing the money to the affected would not work. Regular and income generating activities were the major needs of the affected. She added that there are different types of conflict affected so all the affected should be treated in a same manner. The conflict affected should be provided compensation and other activities as per their need (IHRC, 2013).

## Pruning and Verification of Real Cases: Necessary

She further connoted that government and responsible authority should go to the real field and understand the real situation of the affected rather than merely making plans and policies sitting in Kathmandu. So the real needs of the affected could be addressed for their livelihood and it would be the real tribute to the person who has lost their lives in the conflict.

## Cross Case Analysis

### *Failures on One and all Commitments*

Even though it was agreed in the CPA that the peace agreement would be concluded* within six months and would introduce long term programs to support and enhance the livelihood of the conflict affected children, it took more than ten years to complete the peace agreement which largely met its objective but failed to address some major concerns of the conflict affected till now. From the beginning of the process, there appeared distinct differences and contradictions of perception of the government of Nepal, political parties and other stakeholders on the affected especially on the education and livelihood of those conflict affected children.

**Table 2: Livelihood After Peace agreement**

| Participants | Support (Gov. and development Organization) | Social Acceptance | Need and Demand |
|---|---|---|---|
| Sarada | - Got first installment of Golden handshake package<br>-Tailoring training | -Community people afraid<br>-Excluded from social work<br>-Not trusted in partnership | -Societal awareness<br>- Some skill related training for livelihood |

| | | | |
|---|---|---|---|
| Mahadev | -Got first installment as a Maoist affected<br>-Got scholarship by Shanti samiti for the brothers and sisters | -Nobody trust to give loan after the death of father | -Justice and punishment<br>-Educational loan<br>-Job<br>-Future sustainability |
| Khim Bahadur | - Got first installment of Golden handshake package<br>-Got basic medical treatment subsidy | - Community people afraid<br>-Excluded from social work<br>-Nobody trust to give loan for medical treatment | --Societal awareness<br>- Financial support for his recuperation<br>- Some skill related training for livelihood<br>-Job guarantee |
| Radhika | - Got some amount of money as a CPN (Maoist) affected<br>- Got scholarship by which is provided by Gov. for the brothers and sisters | - Nobody trust to give loan for her grandmother and mother medical treatment<br>- Nobody trust to give loan for her brother and sister education | - Justice and punishment<br>- Financial support for her grandmother and mother recuperation<br>-Suggests the government to find the real affected and provide relief program<br>-Life related skill based training<br>-Job guarantee |

## Non-Acceptance as Ordinary Member

From the interview of the participants, it was known that the community had not accepted Sarada as an ordinary member because of her background of the CPN (Maoist) party. She chose the option of voluntary retirement from the CPN (Maoist) cantonment and wanted to invest the money provided at the time of retirement. But there were several hurdles in the society to accept her as a member in the society as she was blamed that she came back after killing several people which was a sinful act. She was excluded in several programs and trainings provided by the development organizations only for being the cadre of the CPN (Maoist) party.

## Claims of Another Participant: Left Unheard

Mahadev was another affected of the CPN (Maoist) party. He was provided some relief for the survival but it was not enough. He could not get the scholarship from the government as mentioned in the CPA as he was above 18 years. He thought the study of his small brother and sister was better than his own, so he held a job. He even didn't get help, loan from his relatives and other people of society for his education. His brothers and sisters also did not get enough money to pay the fee on time and were often excluded from the class. Recently, he was also doing private B.Ed. as a part time student and helping his family with his job. Also sometimes, he faced several difficulties in the college for not paying the college fee as he was not getting good salary, and not on time. Though he was not getting appropriate job as per his qualification as he had no one to help for the career opportunity. He raised demand some educational loan for the affected like him who wished to continue their study. And the government should be responsible in providing education to the affected children till they wish to study and also provide them with a secured job. He was also seeking justice to punish the murderer of his father.

## Help and Support of Avocation Growth: Throw in Diustbin

Khim Bahadur was another affected of the conflict. He got the voluntary retirement from the CPN (Maoist) party as he was wounded in the war and his arm had some problems. He got one third amount of the money by the government for the retirement and with that money, he tried medical treatment for his injury but the amount was insufficient. He even asked for loan but couldn't receive it as his treatment was costly and would take some years for recovery. His mother was also treated as a widow in the society and was not treated well in different social programs, festivals, rituals. Khim Bahadur was also treated in the same way. His disappeared brother is still unknown; whether he is dead or alive even after 10 years of the CPA. With the social exclusion and bad treatment of the society, he would sometimes think of going abroad or migrating but his mother did not want so. Also he did not have enough money to invest to go abroad. For further career development, he did not have adequate qualification so he was unable to apply to different vacancies. He even could not study as his age did not support him to join the small brothers and sisters in school. Besides, he had the responsibility to take care of his mother and small kids of his big brother. So he was seeking some help and support for income generating activities.

## Hundreds Father are Still at Large

Radhika, an innocent girl was affected by the job of her father in the security force of the nation. After the murder of her father by the CPN (Maoist) party, she has been struggling for the justice of her father and to punish the criminals. Her voices were however not heard by the authentic bodies of the government as she did not have anyone in that field. The people who have killed her father are still at large but no one would bother to care about her sufferings. The situation after her father's death could not help her to continue the study so she left school and started to advocate for justice. Her grandmother and mother were still not fully recovered by the traumatic event. So she needed to take care of them and help in other household activities. The money provided as the compensation was not enough for their survival. But she had seen that the fake affected of the armed conflict were getting a lot of money by using the political power. She was feeling guilty of seeing those acts and raised question whether there was the government or not. She was neither able to continue her study nor help the family members fully. So she demanded the nation to fulfill the basic needs of the affected. She even did not have money to buy a cetamol for her grandmother and mother treatment was far away for her. So she was facing a pitiful situation and seeking help for the sustainable livelihood by involving her in some income generating activities.

## Miserable Condition of All Conflict Affected Children

In conclusion, the situation of the conflict affected children in the post conflict situation is also miserable. In the conflict era they were out of the mainstream of education and in the post conflict situation they are in the stage of fulfilling the needs of their family so education is not the major agenda for them. Only Mahadev is able to continue the education even though he is also facing several problems and challenges. On the other hand, the government is not providing adequate help and facilities for the affected of the conflict. The participants have faced several hindrances in the society just being the affected of the armed conflict. In absence of the main person of the home, they are not getting loan and help from the people of the society as there is no one to pay the loan back. They even do not have a capsule when they and their family members fall ill. To add to their plight, their relatives captured their land and property after the death of the children's parents. Sometimes, the subsidy is also taken by the relatives in their name. Also the real affected are not getting enough help as the fake affected are taking the relief amount by using the political power. The compensation amount is also not used in the proper way as no one is helping and trusting them for doing some income generating activities. Their academic qualification and lack of political power are the problems for not getting a proper job. During the war, they are being affected of the conflict mentally but in the present situation, they are more affected by the poverty and the behavior of the people around them. So the major choice of the affected children is of getting help for the sustainable livelihood to take care of their family rather than getting formal education.

## Summary of the Chapter

This chapter primarily deals with the conflict affected school going children's experiences of adversities caused by the armed conflict in post conflict suitation. The interview with the particpiants shows that ten years armed conflict had lasting impacts on the physical, psychological, and socioeconomic well-being on those school going children. Due to the cause of the conflict, they have abysmal situation in the post conflict situation as well. Though they were provided support, it was designed with minimal or no consultation with the affected groups and hence, do not adequately reflect the needs of the affected children and their living. It means that, there are requirements of different types of support as per these affected demand. The major demand of the affected children is to enhance their economic status by fulfilling the basic needs.

## Following Quotation is Work Perusal

If secretary, physician and preceptors, are none but only forge! Ruler patients and learners proceed nowhere, but drowned in Gorge. Anonymous.

# 6

# Findings and Discussion

## What's e* inside? Two Questions

This section of my research includes the findings in response to the two research questions posed in the beginning of this study. The first question focused on exploring the experiences of the school going children during the period of ten years armed conflict. The second question aimed to delving into those children's experiences of adversities caused by armed conflict in their everyday life at present. It furthermore explores, what support they are receving from the state and non-state actors including their family/community in their efforts towards their livelihood in the post conflict situation. Hence, in this chapter; the findings based on the interview with the participants are included. On the basis of the findings, the discussions have been made. The discussion is based on the participants' responses along with the literatures rclated to my study. And the reflections of the findings are presented in a critical way. For this, the past studies and the theory are interlinked.

## Findings

From the study, it was now exfacieknown that the school going children were being affected by both the state and the CPN (Maoist) party. The participants were neither being protected as child when they were school going children nor were they protected after being the affected. Participants were either engaged in the CPN (Maoist) party and or affected for not supporting the CPN (Maoist) party.

The reason behind they left school were because of (i) the extreme poverty, (ii) social discrimination based on caste, gender, (iii) parents' profession, (iv) different political ideology, and (v) torture etc. Some participants participated in the armed conflict in the CPN (Maoist) party due to their parents' involvement and regular torture by the state security forces. Whereas some participants became the affected as their parents were the government employeres i.e. teacher and Nepal army respectively and didn't obey the decision of leaving the job and supporting the CPN (Maoist).

## District Pains – Different Ways of Solution

After the peace agreement, the participant got voluntary-retirement who was engaged in the CPN (Maoist) party and other was waiting for justice. They have registered the case and were waiting for justice and peace by providing punishment for the criminals who killed their parents. The social acceptance of the affected in the society was the major challenge and still it existed. The society had not accepted the CPN (Maoist) combatants after the peace agreement as they were considered to be the sinful persons coming back by killing people. Likewise, those who were affected by the CPN (Maoist) were not getting help and security from the members of their society. All participants had become the main breadwinner in their families. All the participants' cases seemed that it was their compulsion to engage in other household activities. Except one participant, all other three were not continuing formal education because fulfilling the basic needs was the major priority for them.

## Nature of Support Alias Relief 0grram

The supports were like the fire bridge – short term solutions. Ex combatants have got 6 lakhs as provision of the self-retirement from the CPN (Maoist) combatants whereas the one got 1 lakh and the other one got 10 lakhs as the compensation of the loss of their father. It was not the exact solution to the real affected ones. Without conducting the need analysis, the support was provided. Some had a very panic situation whereas some had a normal situation. So the same support was not suitable for all the affected. "One size doesn't fit all" exactly suits the situation of the conflict affected.

The present situation of the conflict affected children was taking care of their old parents, brothers, sisters so they were unable to continue education except one participant. All of the other had left the formal education and were in the need of some income generating activities through trainings, loans and job.

## Discussion

Clues he discussions are based on the findings of the study. The findings have been discussed with related literatures.

### School Going Children: Affected by Armed Conflict

There are many reasons for using children who are under age of 18 in the armed conflict by the armed groups. Because of children's psychological and physically immaturity, because of their lack of independence, because they rarely analyze the risk the school going children were taken in conflict. Also they require less food than adult fighter and are much easier to train and force into becoming aggressive, because of their age and inherent innocence, they are perceive as less threatening which is useful in confusing the adversities. Not only this, children who are living in conflict areas, the experience of direct physical or structural violence lead the children to get into the armed group.

## Difference Reason for Being Affected

During the conflict era, many students became the affected of the armed conflict. There are different reasons for being affected from both sides. The reasons that the participants of the study became affected in the ten years armed conflict are:

## Socio-Economic, Cultural Practices: Exploitation of Children in Armed Conflict

Use of children in armed conflict is not a new phenomenon in the world. Various literatures show that the massive numbers of children under the age of 18 are used in armed conflicts. Children are used in over thirty countries, including Myanmar, Colombia, Uganda, Ethiopia, Sudan, Somalia, Liberia and Democracy Republic of Congo by armed force and government as well (Czyz, 2008). Similarly, Center for Defense Information Colombia (2001) stated that armed groups also target children for forcible recruitment by showing children surrounding problems in their force in Colombia. Similarly, the socio economic condition, discrimination, poverty etc. are addressed by the political parties and the children are engaged in the armed conflict which was not addressed by the existing government (Gautam, 2007; Pradhan 2012). In the study of the United Nations Children Fund (2003), it shows that, "Children are the most susceptible to recruitment by manipulation alluring or may be driven to join armed forces and groups because of poverty or discrimination" (p. 5). Often they are abducted at school, on the streets or at home. So children are not safe and secure in the conflict period. Similarly, the children are the eye witness of the abduction, torture and social crime by the both parties. This led the feelings of revenge and they are compelled to choose either one side or another side and became affected.

### *Psychological and Physical Immaturity Exploited*

The CPN (Maoist) party used the children as they are emotional and could do anything what they are told to do. Children are targeted due to their psychological and physical immaturity, also because of their lack of independence, ignorant of their rights; they are helpless and particularly vulnerable to being taken advantage of (ICRC, 2011).In my study, Sarada has the same situation and almost similar reasons for being the member of the CPN (Maoist) party. They are because of the extreme poverty, social discrimination based on caste; gender etc.

### Witness of Crime by Security Force

Khim was being affected as he was the witness of the abduction and sexual abuse of his family by the state security force. That means when children feel helpless and injustice; suffered from poverty, and excluded in the society they perceive joining armed groups as a way of escaping danger and gaining some sort of security and justice (Nilsson, 2005).

### Poverty and Torture

Normally children's recruitment into non-state armed groups has been viewed as a result of poverty, family violence, torture and lack of education (Burgress, 2009).This torture and recruitment of children is illegal in Nepal under Article 7 of the Children's Act. Because of no ability to adjust in the tortured situation, social exclusion and extreme poverty, these two participants joined the CPN (Maoist) party and left the study thinking that the revolution would end all kinds of social discriminations.

### Different Political Ideology and Profession

Not only the poverty and social discrimination, there are other reasons too for the affected of the armed conflict. The reasons of being affected differ as the parties are different for making children affected. The ten years armed conflict was started by the CPN (Maoist). And the people who do not support them and have different political ideology from theirs are all the enemies for them. So the people different from them are being affected in different ways. The teachers, government officials, security forces, people from other parties and public had faced the unbearable threaten, physical punishment and even killed in a very simple matter of doing rejection of their decisions, not helping them, not paying demanded money (Gautam, 2007). The government officials were even threatened to leave their job and join the CPN (Maoist) party. And if the officials do not obey, there are several cases of killing those officials from the CPN (Maoist).

## Those Affected by CPN (Maoist) Party

Similarly, in my study, Mahadev and Radhika were affected by the CPN (Maoist) party. It was because the family members were not the supporters of the party, not providing money, not leaving the job of the state security force and they were conveying the message to the army personnel about them. They have lost their family members for not obeying what the people of CPN (Maoist) party were saying. So with the regular torture and the responsibility to take care of the family members after the death of the main person of the family, these two participants had been the affected of the conflict and were compelled to leave their study.

## Affected by Both – State and CPN (Maoist) Party

According to the participants' stories, it was known that the conflicts affected were being affected by both the state and the CPN (Maoist) party. Though there are several child conventions and rules, regulations, protocols for the child right protection even in armed conflict time, they were not seen practically in the study area. The participants were neither being protected as child when they were school going children nor were they protected after being the affected. School building: An easy resort also the children who were tortured by both the state and the CPN (Maoist) party were leaving school education as they did not find the secured life in school and way to school (Gautam, 2007). Also the schools were taken as battleground, in rural areas the schools were only substantial permanent buildings by the state security forces and CPN (Maoist) used as indoctrination programs and rallies (Gautam, 2007). In this way, the situation tended the children to be affected and compelled them to quit school as the school did not have good environment.

## Both State and Maoist * Commitments

Neither the state nor the CPN (Maoist) fulfilled the commitments that are demanded by the child conventions (Advocacy Forum Nepal, 2006).The state security forces were also torturing the students who were under the age of 18 and the CPN (Maoist) party was also recruiting the children who were under the age of 18 in the war. So it seemed that none of the sides were fulfilling the commitments. It was the compulsion for the school going children to catch a gun and fight against the people in the society who have discriminated them. Also the children were being the main persons after the death of the breadwinner of the family. All the participants' cases seemed that it was the compulsion to leave school and get engaged in other household activities. Except Mahadev, other three did not continue the formal education because fulfilling the basic needs was the major priority for them.

## Deprived or Education and Compel to Face Challengs

All the circumstances during the conflict have resulted in children to be deprived of the light of education and they have been facing several challenges in the present situation. It has finally resulted in high impact on the process of development of the children who have been affected by the armed conflict. This has directly pulled the development process down and the affected children have missed the educational achievement, and faced different trauma and stress.

## Livelihood After Peace Agreement: Insufficient Relief Support

Conflict is taken as a means of revolution and peace process as the ends of the conflict. It has really resulted in a positive symptom to the conflict affected in the context of Nepal. The CPA (2006) has made some provisions and policies to provide relief and justice for the conflict affected. The major achievements of the CPA were the golden handshake for the PLA and financial support for the affected. Moreover, the conflict affected children were also provided scholarship. Different I/NGOs also helped the conflict affected by providing some packages, scholarship and relief programs like short terms vocational trainings, loan etc. Also the participants have said that the materials are distributed not as per the demand and need of the participants.

## Lack of Fair Judgements

Even they didn't get the exact justice after the peace agreement. But from the participant's story, it is seen that though they are helped in different ways for the reintegration in the society, society hasn't accepted the conflict affected in proper way. The support, needs and the present scenario of the participants after the peace agreement are highlighted below:

> Self-retirement and search of justice. The only way to end the armed conflict is through the discussions, meetings and agreement. If we see the international trend, different countries have adopted different models of the peace

agreement. One of the most used models for the peace agreement is disarmament, demobilization and reintegration (DDR) of soldiers, which should be an integral part of the humanitarian relief and peace building strategy. Thus, in the post-conflict phase, the emphasis should be on reintegration of the former child soldiers to avoid their return to armed groups and do criminal activities in the society.

## A Glimpse of Acts After Peace Agreement

Knowing this reality, after the peace agreement, the CPN (Maoist) combatants were provided options to live in a normal life and the other people affected by the CPN (Maoist) were provided some help and support. Even after the peace agreement, fight for the justice has continued. The self-retirement was the compulsion for the participants to follow the CPA. Whereas fighting for the justice was for providing punishment for the criminals. Article 5.2.5 of the CPA specifically calls for a Truth and Reconciliation Commission to be established in order to "probe about those involved in serious violation of human rights and crime against humanity and develop an atmosphere for reconciliation in society."

## Different Options as Also Choice of Voluntary Retirement

The children who are being the affected in the conflict time in one or another way have returned to the society doing various positive and negative roles. The ex-combatants need to be given various new roles in the society which help them to achieve the equivalent prestige and acknowledge their positive roles that they have done during the armed conflict (Nilsson, 2005). So the ex-combatants are given different options and the study participants have chosen self-retirement.

## Provisions for Reintegration

There are several provisions for the affected of the armed conflict to reintegrate them in the society. Fully repairing affected from the atrocities of the armed conflict is impossible, but acknowledging suffering, restoring affected lives, and strengthening respect for rights are crucial tasks in transitional societies (Miano, 2013). Though the rights and justice are highlighted in the implementation of the CPA but the negligible attention is seen in regards to the affected children. The children being the affected of the armed conflict deserve different justice as recognition for harms suffered, protection of their rights, and access to reparative resources (Miano, 2013).

## Human Rights – Neglected

In the study area, the participants were feeling the same situation as their rights were neglected. The reintegration of the children as self-retirement was the compulsion for Sarada and Khim. They had no option to choose rather than self-retirement as they had injuries and thus were not physically fit. Further, they also had the responsibility to take care of the family members who have been waiting for their retirement for a long time. So they are compelled to return to their homes. I think the need analysis is lacking in this aspect which has been neglected in many reintegration processes and resulted in ex-combatants engaging in markets with little economic potential (Nübler, 1997). If their interest were asked when designing such options for the CPN (Maoist) PLA then it would be better. So individual-based approaches allow for more tailored responses, collective reparations simplify delivery and can reach more people.

## Political Instability: Implementation Distorted

Similarly, Mahadev and Radhika are waiting for justice for their fathers. Though the provision of forming a TRC and providing the justice to those killed and disappeared is mentioned in the CPA by punishing the responsible person for the killing and making disappeared, the implementation is very weak. Because of the political instability, the implementation seems shallow. The people who are engaged in such activities from the CPN (Maoist) party are freely doing their activities being a political person and the security forces who are blamed as criminals are having higher posts and promotion which really show that the crime is being promoted by these types of activities. This has resulted in the society that lacks peace and harmony.

## Safety and Security - Jeopardised

Though the peace agreement has made many provisions on behalf of the conflict affected, the exact scenario in the real field seemed different. The participants had only options of self-retirement. And also the affected still are searching justice which was clearly mentioned in the peace agreement. It shows that the provisions are not as per the need and interest of the affected and it was top bottom approach. So it helped in some aspects but not fulfilled the need of the affected. The affected are still seeking justice and waiting for the time to punish the criminals. So whatever the peace agreement and the concerning stakeholder's committed for the conflict affected, the problem is still there in the real field. The affected are not feeling safe and secure. They are still waiting the day to punish the criminals.

Support provided: Different countries which are highly affected by the armed conflict and participated in the peace agreement have different strategies for providing support to the affected of the conflict. In this regard, Nilsson (2005) stated that:

"Support to ex-combatants is only warranted if -

a) they constitute a security threat to the new peace order,

b) the atrocities that ex-combatants may have committed can create conflict-generating rifts in society, or

c) certain categories of ex-combatants cannot support themselves due to economic, political, or social marginalization. (p. 93)

It shows that the conflict affected may get different threats and challenges after the peace agreement so the support is provided to the affected. Similarly, after the peace agreement in Nepal, the CPA has also helped the affected to get support at different levels.

## Consequences of Less Support: Predicted

The participants have got support from different sources. The government has provided 6 lakhs as the self-retirement for the combatants to reintegrate them in the society. Also the participants got 1 lakh and 10 lakhs as mentioned in the provision for the members of killed and disappeared. The aim of providing the money is to provide short term basic needs for the societal process. And if their needs are not fulfilled and not taken seriously, ex-combatants may re-engage in violence and render post-war reconstruction and peace building impossible (Nilsson, 2005). Also it is for developing harmony, maintain peace, and acculturation in the society. The study showed that there was not provided adequate help and support to the conflict affected. But it would be very shameful in saying that the support programs were also taken by some of the powerful people. The participants who got self-retirement got the amount that is declared by the Nepal government. And the affected from the CPN (Maoist) party are also getting some amount as help. But both the help are not adequate. Also some development partners are providing some help but the fake affected have got more help than the real affected. Khim and Sarada have faced the same case and aren't satisfied with the organizations help too. Donors have often used education and training programs as a way to "buy" time for peace agreements (Nilsson, 2005). This shows that most of the programs are donor driven which lacks the need of the affected.

## An Analysis or Short and Long Term Programs

The urgent need of long term programs is seen for the affected for their sustainable livelihood. The short term programs are not sufficient. Similarly, the help from different organizations is also just the showing piece, but it was known that many relief programs are grasped by the fake affected with the power. The programs are often implemented in a fragile post-conflict environment with tensions and violence (Watson, 2009) which is also seen in Nepal as it is caused because of the political instability, political bargaining between the different parties. So in the present situation also, they are dealt with different perspectives. The reintegration in the society is still a challenge.

## Biased Distribution or Relief: Basic Cause or Dissatisfaction

The supports provided are not distributed equally for all the affected. The case of being affected is different but the pain is same, the loss of the parents is same but the support was provided differently in the same cases. If we see the case of the participants, both of the participants had lost their parents but the way of getting the support is different. It clearly shows that the government and concerning officials, departments are seen bias in this matter. The unequal distribution of the support has created chaos in the society and the affected are also not satisfied in this aspect.

Acceptance of the society: void response seen: Though the participants have got some money for the survival, the social acceptance has still been a challenge for them. Bloomfield, Barnes and Huyse (2003) suggested three basic stages for social reconciliation for the affected of the armed conflict. The first stage is, Replacing Fear by Non-Violent Coexistence, the second stage is When Fear No Longer Rules: Building Confidence and Trust and the third stage is Towards Empathy. But in the context of conflict affected children, none of them is seen.

The present situation of the conflict affected is very miserable. And it would be out of imagination when we talk about the situation that they have actually been facing after the peace agreement.

## Biased Treatment to Affected People

The acceptance of the affected in the society was the major challenge and still it exists. After returning as self-retirement from the PLA of the CPN (Maoist) army force, Sarada and Khim got very severe situation. They were not easily accepted by the society and the societal reintegration was very difficult for them. This showed that cultural contexts, and 'social ecology' (Betancourt & Khan, 2008) are likely to be very important in developing any kind of supportive and acceptable environment, for highly distressed conflict affected children.

## Distinct and Different Social Views

The society looks at them from different lenses. Society blamed them as such returned people by killing several other innocent people and they are sinful people. With these types of different blames and exclusion in different senses in the different religious, social activities, the affected of the conflict are being more affected by the people of the society. They themselves regret on why they are in such a society. They have participated in the war to change the society but still the society is the same. In this aspect, Watson (2009) has also concluded that reintegration is a difficult and lengthy process, mainly because it involves helping ex –combatants and affected people of the armed conflict to move away from the positions that defined them during the conflict to identifying themselves as citizens and members of the local communities, societies (p. 6).

This may be one reason why Sarada and Khim were facing difficulties to reintegrate and adjust in their society in the post conflict situation. They were not getting their exact roles and responsibilities in the society that they used to get in the armed conflict.

## Death of Winners Family: Major Cause of Pain

Similarly, Mahadev and Radhika were being affected by the death of their breadwinners of the family. So the responsibility has been transferred to them. After the death of their parents they were also excluded in the society saying that it was all because of the fate and the people are not good. Even their family members were not taken easily in the society and their grandmother was blamed as witch. Within the society also, different social groups and organizations neglected the participant's social acceptance (International Crisis Group, 2010). Moreover, the society has not accepted the affected as the social members because of the shame, social values, honor and their involvement in the conflict for killing people (Afshar & Eade, 2004). Until and unless the social acceptance is not taken positively, the peace agreement cannot be successful as it may be a matter of revenge and conflict.

## Neglected by Society and Relatives

The conflict affected children are not even helped by the society and the relatives. It is because the children are coming back from the conflict as ex combatants; and some others as the breadwinners since they lost their fathers and were poor. Offering support such as training and employment opportunities, have the potential to contribute to a reduction in previous socio-economic exclusion of some (Watson, 2009). So the affected frustration in the society should be acknowledged and understood by the people of the society with social acceptance. Designing and implementing targeted economic projects for the conflict affected, and actively involving the local private sector in the implementation of projects that have the potential to boost up local economies which will ensure benefits helps to assure the social acceptance of the conflict affected (Watson, 2009) that is lacking in the context of Nepal. So this shows that the participation of the conflict affected children in different projects for the economic benefit along with the local communities and local business persons, local private sectors will also help them to get social acceptance.

## Compulsion: Major Cause for Joining Conflict

Engaging in conflict was the compulsion. It was by different reasons that are within the society. And reintegration in the society is still a challenge for the participants. It seems that the awareness programs are not conducted in the society. The people of the society are still in the mentality of fear of the war as they are the real eye witness of the torture, threaten, murder of their relatives, neighbors of the society. So still the mindset of the people has not changed and they still have the feelings that the affected of war are also the criminals. So they are taking them as the sinful. And they still have fear. So they are not involved in social activities. Similarly, CPN (Maoist) cadres are also showing the political affinity and still have revenge on the people who have different political ideology. So, it seems that the social harmony is not seen in the society. It is an urgent need to maintain social harmony among the people in the society and the conflict affected through different programs in the help of civil society.

## Education After the Peace Agreement: Next After Livelihood

Regarding the educational status that they wanted to continue, all the participants have said that education was not their first priority as they were having the main responsibility of making a livelihood. Among four, only Mahadev was continuing his education but not in an easy way; he was suffering from economic crisis. And other three did not want to continue their education, mostly because of the age bar (as they perceived). The students who were in the schools are like small brothers and sisters and it would be difficult for them to study with them. And also the economic problem is there for continuation of their study. They also said that in the time of catching pen on hands, they fought for the freedom of the country with a gun in their hands.

## Whom Need Education: The Most

So again returning to school after a long time would not help them for good achievement. But it is known that the one who wants to study should be provided the environment and the ones who are taking care of the small brothers and sisters should be helped in their education so as to ensure better jobs for future. Employment in the civil services is often not feasible for uneducated ex-combatants children and conflict affected (Watson, 2009). But if we see the case of Namibia and Zimbabwe, though they did not have adequate education the conflict affected were rewarded with the public posts. UN (1999) also focused on providing suitable recruitment of the conflict affected though they were having low or no education and being unskilled. But this situation is not seen in the context of Nepal. The children affected are asked to have required qualification for the job in different sectors. So, for them not getting required education is one of the obstacles to be engaged in job.

## Challenges and Problems: Major Hurdles

The participant's educational aspect is in shadow as they have other major challenges and problems to face. Though the educational rights are provided to the conflict affected (Akiyode Afolabi, 2013), three affected ignored it as they had other responsibilities to fulfill. The ignorance was obvious as they did not have other option to fulfill the basic needs. They have been the breadwinners of the family and it was difficult for them to continue their education. If the government provided full scholarship, full guarantee of the future and help to fulfill the basic needs of the family, then only they could continue their education.

## Present situation and their need: Need Analysis not done

The supports are like the fire bridge. They were not the exact solution for the real affected. Without the need analysis, the support was provided. Some have very panic situation whereas others have a normal situation. So the same support cannot suitable for all the affected. Mahadev was asking for the educational loan but he is not getting it. In this aspect, UN (1999) stated:

> "Former combatants, conflict affected however, almost always lack the necessary capital to get started after the peace agreement and have bleak prospects of securing loans from private banks. Donors and government agencies must therefore assist in giving ex-combatants access to favorable credit schemes. (p. 81)"

## Miscellaneous Circumstances to Cope With

Apart from this, Khim was asking for help for the treatment of his parents, Sarada was asking for help for getting training for income generating activities and Radhika is asking for help for the treatment of old grandmother and mother and her livelihood. So the analysis of the need of the affected should be done. Without the need analysis of the affected any programs conducted from the government and the development organizations would not be successful, which is a good lesson that could be learnt from the support distribution to the affected of the study area. The best way of doing this is to provide ex-combatants with meaningful occupations whereby they can support themselves and their families (Spear, 2002).

## Sustainable Livelihood: The First & Foremost Need

Getting education was not the prior need of the conflict affected, but the sustainable livelihood was the prior need. Likewise, the help provided by the state and other development organizations were not sufficient. The affected raise their voices on the long term programs for the affected. For this, they have raised the voices for getting some skill based training so that they could do something on their own. The study of Spear (2002) also highlighted that the need of different training and skill base programs is more appropriate for conflict affected people. He added that access to training for the conflict affected is especially important in countries with advanced economies, where the inconsistency between the skills that ex-combatants possess and the skills that are in demand on the labor market is the greatest (p. 145).

## A Suitable and Appropriate Step for Support

This shows that the need analysis and understanding of the job market is to be assessed and the education or training is to be provided to the affected of the armed conflict. But in the case of Nepal it has not been done so the affected are not satisfied with the support that they are getting and demanding the vocational training as per their need, but not as a compulsion. Vocational training has traditionally been seen as the best way for ex-combatants to acquire skills in areas such as plumbing, masonry, carpentry, electrical work, and small scale cottage industry (Nilsson, 2005). But in Angola, apprenticeships were more effective than vocational training, because skills and income were acquired more quickly by the conflict affected (Verhey, 2002). So the status and the capabilities of the affected also need to be understood.

## Life Skill and Help for Starting the Works

The participants have an urgent need of income generating activities. So for this they demanded to get some life skills and help for starting the work. Trainings on vocational skills done via apprenticeships must be based on proper labor market studies and be demand driven (Nübler, 1997). But if we see the participant's story then the trainings and help were not demand driven but were laden as compulsion without any options. So the need based analysis and market studies have often been lacking in many reintegration efforts sponsored by donors (Steenken & Thorgren, 2004). And the responsible authority should listen to the voices of the voiceless to fulfill the urgent demands. In conclusion, school going children are particularly vulnerable in the post conflict situation in Nepal. Although the short term supports and remedies have tried to reduce the present suffering somehow but there are worries about future. So it is essential to take necessary steps to address their agenda as soon as possible.

## Miserable Situation Still Prevailing

So for various reasons, the conflict affected children are facing miserable situation at present as well. Hart (n.d.) also said that the disappearance, imprisonment and the death of the family members affect the post conflict situation. It is because of poverty, lack of education for suitable job, loss of their parents, caring for the old parents, brothers and sisters. It has caused social, economic, psychological, physical effects on the conflict affected children in the post conflict situation. This is because most of the development focused strategies are emotion based and short term but the need of the conflict affected children is problem focused which has been effective in different countries (Paardekooper, 2002). If we see the country specific scenario, the victims who are severely affected by the conflict are slightly changing their livelihood and the societal harmony. It shows that the participants have the ability to absorb the pains and maintain harmony within the society after the painful situation, which is highlighted in resilience theory. So, resilience is maintaining the positive peace in terms of social structure, order, feedbacks and relationships within the member of the society after being involved in any kind of conflict.

## Residence: Highlighted

So resilience is the process of being well-being in the society and returning in their previous situation. Time and again, the participants of the study are returning in the normal life, has been recovered from the trauma of the conflict. Resilience theory also describes that the stressful experiences turns into positive adaptation (Masten 1994, as cited in Luthar, Cicchetti, & Becker, 2000). And the same situation is seen in the practices of school going children affected and their turnover of the life in positive adaptation in the present context.

## Present Needs Peeping in Baloney of Fulfillment

Also the present needs of the conflict affected children are fulfilling the basic needs, getting justice, some skill based training for income generation and sustainable job for the sustainable future which is also included in ICRC (2009). The present need of the conflict affected children is for the positive adjustment, recovery of the painful situation to maintain peace in the society which will ultimately led them to gain the productive life as resilience theory suggests. So the necessity of the conflict affected can be fulfilled by providing vocational education for them as per their needs (Devkota, 2015) which helps them to participate in the income generating activities for their livelihood and the future. Thus, only after the economic achievement, they could maintain the social, political and psychological achievement in the society for the social acceptance and then create social harmony and peace.

## Two Aspects of Solution

If we see from the perspective of resilience theory, the present adversities and fulfilling the affected children's needs will help to maintain positive peaceful environment in the society and secure their individual life.

The participants have said that the conflict affected should be provided the relief package through need analysis. And the needs of the affected for the children are the income generating activities which are directed to skill based training. There are no choices for them so the same relief packages are provided for them which are not suitable as per their need (Devkota, 2015). In this regards if the choices are provided for them then they could select the perfect package which would lead for sustainable livelihood for them.

## Views of Amartya Sen: An Awardee of Nobel Prize

Amartya Sen has also focused on the freedom of choices for the development of the individual. Sen's Capabilities Approach (1993) focuses that capability is the freedom to achieve valuable beings and doings. So understanding this reality, if the participant's capability is applied to provide the support and the help for the affected children, then it would have become better in the survival of their livelihood. The main theme of the capability approach is the distinction between the means and the ends of well-being and development.

## Significance of Sen's Approach

Sen's approach suggests that every individual has their own abilities and if they are mastered then there would be several choices to move ahead. It also focuses on the affected centered approaches rather than centralized approach for supporting affected needs. It also focuses that only the ends have intrinsic importance, whereas means are only instrumental to reach the goal of increased well-being and development. In our context, the affected are only provided the means which is insufficient and they are in search of ends for the sustainable livelihood. Sen (1993) stressed on the role of agency, the process of choice and the freedom to reason in the selection of relevant capabilities. But the role of agency is not seen in proper amount for the choices and freedom of selecting the relevant capabilities of the affected. So the issues should be focused on providing choices.

## Elimination or Poverty: The First Need

The problem behind the situation of the conflict affected children was to solve the hand to mouth problem after the demise of the main person (head) of the family. So poverty matters them. And the reasons behind these problems need an urgent solution on the base of need assessment. In this regard, Sen (1999) stated poverty as sensibly identified in terms of capability deprivation. In this regards, he suggested that poverty situation can be improved by focusing not only on generating economic growth but by enhancing people's intrinsically important capabilities. The same situation is in the conflict affected children of Nepal. Though some support was provided, it did not help to develop them intrinsically. The supports were just like the seed money, short term based and fixed for all the cases. But the needs of the participants to cope with the present situation were different. The provided supports are also not adequate and used in proper way by different circumstances. So they are facing several problems in the society, especially in regards with their livelihood.

The affected have no more choices. They are limited with the support provided by the state and some development organizations. So they are not able to do as per their needs and interests which has resulted in capacity deprivation and increased poverty in the post conflict situation.

## Freedom of Choices for Employment

Sen (1997) focused on the freedom of choices with alternative combinations of functioning for their life contributes to reducing poverty, enhancing the capability and balancing the power structure. Agreeing with Sen's perspective, I believe that poverty and capability matter most in using the potentials of conflict affected children and they are struggling for reintegration. So if more choices were provided to the participants they could choose the best options which would fit for them to develop their capacity which will finally lead to sustainable social and economic life.

## Need Analysis and Immediate Support: Expected

With the resilience theory and capability approach, it is seen that the participants are recovering their traumatic life but not as per their abilities. If the participants are helped as per their abilities, needs and interests they could have good recovery to get the productive life and it could be more effective. I can say that only after fulfilling their demands with the needs analysis and freedom of choices, the livelihood of the conflict affected children would be sustainable and peace agreement will have a successful ending.

## Summary of the Chapter

This chapter provided the key findings and discussions on the basis of data analysis and interpretation with reference to each of the research questions. The findings were based on the participant's interview and the discussions were based on the findings and literatures. And I have included my views as critical reflection in the discussions. The participants were the children under the age of 18 years who were involved in the conflict for various reasons like poverty, social exclusion, discrimination, revenge which has made them to left the school education. After the peace agreement, they got some support from the government but still are not getting social reintegration and they are fighting for social justice and punishment for the criminals. Leaving their formal education when they were under 18 has resulted in unemployed now, when they are above 18since they don't have adequate education in one hand and on the other hand, they have responsibility of taking care and fulfilling the basic needs of the family. So their present need for the sustainable future can be met through vocational education and educational loans or help.

# 7

# Summary, Conclusions and Implications

## An Ultimate Gem of Sea-Churning

This chapter summarizes the whole findings of the study. It also concludes with the findings based on the interview regarding the school going children's experiences of conflict and the adversities that they are facing in their daily life in the post conflict situation. Moreover it focuses on the time from when the children became affected and how they came up to the present condition of their social reintegration. This chapter also indicates how the study will be helpful for the future researchers, policy makers, educators and conflict experts. So this chapter mainly focuses on the summary of the collected data, conclusions based on the findings and summary and the experience, knowledge and reflection on the entire process are highlighted as implications of the study.

## Summary

The issue of conflict affected children is discussed very often by a range of people in different arena may it be in regards to education, relief programs, or sustainable livelihood. But the exact implementation model has still not been able to fulfill the needs of the affected. In the context of Nepal, from the primary data, the conflict affected who were children (under the age of 18) during the ten years armed conflict time are not getting the effective ways out ahead.

During the conflict, the school going children faced several problems in the society. The poverty, discrimination in the society and search for justice were considered to lead the participants to join the CPN (Maoist) party and leave school. In this aspect, the parents' involvement in the CPN (Maoist) party and the torture to the children by the state security forced them to join the CPN (Maoist) party. This case was applicable to Sarada and Khim Bahadur. Whereas, Mahadev and Radhika had been the affected because of their parents' involvement in the political parties different from the Moist and being the officials of the state's security force respectively. It clearly shows that who are against the CPN (Maoist) and the state security forces were being affected by both the sides. Without getting good environment to continue their study and the responsibility to fulfill all the needs of the family after losing the breadwinner of the family, they have left school education.

## Education Addressed as Bourgeois by Maoists

Not only this, the children who were involved in the CPN (Maoist) party also compelled to leave school as the main agenda was to address the problems that they were suffering in the society. And the education was termed as "*bourgeois*" (education for the elites) so many schools were padlocked. It seemed that the main reasons behind leaving the education during the conflict time were that the children themselves were being affected. It was clearly known from the interview that the rights of the children were totally neglected in the conflict, by both the forces.

## Both (State Supported and Maoist Supported) are in Pain

In one or another way, the children were being affected of the conflict but still the situation has not been fair for the affected children.

The children who joined the CPN (Maoist) party have got self-retirement from the PLA after the CPA which provided them with some amount of money but it was not sufficient for them to make a sustainable livelihood. And the children who had been affected from the CPN (Maoist) party are still in search of help for the sustainable livelihood. They got some amount of money as scholarship till the age under 18. But the participants have come up age and education was not the priority for them. The support of 10 lakhs that the PLA got was insufficient to fulfill the present needs of the family. And they also do not have jobs at present so it became more difficult. Mahadev who has a job was is in difficult situation as he is serving as father in the family and have to pay the fee of the small brothers and sisters, and fulfill the basic needs of the family. So the support provided was not effective and sufficient.

## Reintegration: A Herculean Task

The affected children got some sort of help for their settlement in the society but reintegration has been difficult for them. Similarly, after the peace agreement, the society still behaves them in a negative way. The retirement from PLA has made the children more affected as they are totally rejected by the people of the society for the actions they did during the war. The people of the society say that members are not treated well. This has really made them sad and they often recall that the problems that they have faced before and during the conflict were not that much difficult as facing the problem of social reintegration in the post conflict situation.

## Society Rigid Conservative: No Reforms Expected

The hope to change the society seemed to have broken, since they found that the society is still the same and poverty still exists in the society. So the livelihood has been a problem for them. The affected are neither educated nor have got some vocational skills and trainings for making a sustainable livelihood. The affected have demanded some long term programs which would help them for income generating activities as the support provided for them was not on the basis of need analysis. It clearly shows that the affected are being more affected in the post conflict situation so the adequate programs like skill based trainings or some programs that help in income generating activities and providing loans to the affected have been most urgent for the affected.

## Conclusions

Not only the children suffer from the direct consequences of ten years armed conflict (recruitment in armed forces or groups, physical injuries, death), but also they were indirectly affected by displacement, loss of relatives and death of family member and the trauma related with witnessing acts of violence. It has psychological impact on the children; they have faced different trauma, stress, depression, frustration. The depressed affected could do suicide (Pradhan, 2012). This not only has harm on the children but also on the society as the children is the future planners.

### A Desire to Take Revenge Arose

Some children who left the school by seeing those problems around them were being crueler to take revenge of those who have created the problem by killing the family members. Akhtar (2002) also emphasized the affected children of the armed conflict as, "affected reverse the power asymmetry between themselves and their perpetrators by taking revenge" (p. 181). This shows that the situation was serious and out of which the feeling of enmity has developed. This has resulted in the end of the academic career of the conflict affected children. The students who are the future planners of the nation are facing such kind of situation. In this aspect, how could the country get the academic human resource for the nation building process, is one of the never ending questions.

## Need of Hour: Adequate Support

If these youths are not given an opportunity to improve their lives especially on economic, they will easily be captivated back into violence, whether urban gangs, illicit business dealings, or rebel militias in armed conflict (ICRC, 2011). Similarly, ten years armed conflict affected children express feelings fears, and uncertainties about returning to their communities of origin and starting new lives from scratch. So they had fewer options to choose and also those options were not as per their abilities. If they have less options and needs are not identified then the support would be only the ends not the means as Amartya Sen highlights.

## Need to Change Social Temperament

The social reintegration has again created another problem for the conflict affected children. Though the conflict has created awareness in the people of the society (Shakya, 2006), the people who have fought for the freedom (children involving in CPN (Maoist) party are neglected by the society. The government has also provided some support on the blanket approach which has not helped them much for the enhancement of the living standards. If we see, the conflict affected children present condition; they are also searching such kind of help for income generation and sustainable livelihood. If they couldn't get such help, it would certainly lead them to criminal activities.

## Core Elements of Reintegration Drive

Following up on vocational training, income-generating activities are a core element of reintegration programs, providing conflict affected children with concrete livelihood opportunities. They enable conflict affected children to start small businesses and avoid returning to the bush, other exploitative and rejoin in armed group. Income-generating activities go beyond ensuring economic survival or improving living conditions. They foster acceptance within the community because they give young people an opportunity to play a productive and valuable role in society. So as per their interest and need, it seems to formulate such kind of programs.

In conclusion, if the voices of the conflict affected are not heard in time by the responsible authorities, there is an equal chance to increase crime in the society. The situation seems more crucial. So without adequate solution to the conflict affected, the peace agreement would not be successful.

## Implications of Ontogeny

After drawing the conclusions of the study, it ultimately provides some good aspects for the policy and practice in the field of the conflict affected children. It would be helpful for the policy makers, educators and future researchers.

## Implications for Policy Makers

If we see the policies and plans for the children in conflict, all the policies and plans are advocating the protection of the child rights during the conflict and resettlement in the society. But the implementation is seen very weak as the children were used in conflict from both sides during the armed conflict and were affected. If the implementation is done by monitoring and evaluation during the different types of conflict, then it results in the low participation of the children who are under 18 in the conflict. The policies are related to the child affected as combatants. If the issues of the children who are affected by other reasons like parents, family, society are addressed then it addresses the need and justice for those children. The targeted approach, affected centric policies through need analysis is urgently needed to address the rights of the affected which are not fulfilled by one door policies. Also for the conflict affected who are only seeking help from the donors, awareness programs for living and building confidence by the policy makers help them to be independent.

## Implications for Conflict Professionals

The conflict of Nepal was believed to have begun to address the social problems in the society which was totally different from the conflict of other countries. So the main agenda was to solve the social problems like extreme poverty, social discrimination, exclusion etc. Understanding the conflict resolution process, by conflict professionals in the context of Nepal helps to make the peace agreement successful. Focusing on local practices of the Nepalese society rather than focusing on the international practices in the context of Nepal for the peace agreement will help more to maintain peace and harmony there. Solving the problems of the surrounding environment of the affected children as the first priority, would help in acculturation. So the professionals can focus on the social reintegration of the conflict affected.

## Implications for Future Researchers

This study was carried out exploring the experiences of the school going children who were affected in the country's ten years long armed conflict (1996 - 2006). So there are many issues that could be covered by the future researchers. The future researchers could do the research on the issues of the children covering different age groups. This research is only focused on the study of the school level children so the perceptions of the affected of the higher level could also be another issue. This study has only covered the educational experiences so the research could be done of other dimensions like social, cultural, economic, environmental, etc. Thus, this study would be a base to conduct other studies.

## Summary of the Chapter

This is the final chapter of the study which comprises the summary, conclusions and implications of the study. I have summarized the study as per the research questions through the primary data. On the basis of the findings the conclusions were drawn. Likewise, on the basis of the conclusion, the implications for the policy makers, professionals of the conflict and the future researchers were mentioned.

# References


Advocacy Forum Nepal. (2006). *Sharing experiences of torture survivors.* Kathmandu, Nepal: Author. Retrieved from http://advocacyforum.org/downloads/pdf/sharing-experiences-of-torture-survivors.pdf

Advocacy Forum and Human Rights Watch. (2011). *Adding insult to injury: continued impunity for was time abuses.* Retrieved from http://www.peace brigades.ch/fileadmin/user_upload/documents/publikationen_pbi_internatioal/adding-insult-to-injury-nov-30-2011-english-version.pdf

Afshar, H., & Eade, D. (2004). *Development, women, and war: Feminist perspectives.* Oxford, England: Oxfam.

Agency for Co-operation Research in Development. (2007). *Alost generation: Young people and conflict in Africa.* Nairobi, Kenya: Author. Retrieved from http://www.acordinternational.org/silo/files/a-lost-generation-young-people-ad-conflict-in-africa.pdf

Akhtar, S. (2002). Forgiveness: Origins, dynamics, psychopathology and technical relevance. *Psychoanalytic Quarterly, 71*, 175-212. Retrieved from http://onlinelibrary.wiley.com/doi/10.1002/j.2167-4086.2002.tb00010.x/pdf

Akiyode Afolabi, A. (2013). *Gender justice in post conflict societies: An assessment of Sierra Leone and Liberia* (Unpublished doctoral thesis). SOAS, University of London, England.

Amnesty International Report. (2005). *Nepal children caught in the conflict.* Retrieved from http://reliefweb.int/sites/reliefweb.int/files/resources/9CFFFA25DDDE7C404925704A000502B0-ai-npl-26jul.pdf

Anderson, R. (1998). Intuitive inquiry: A transpersonal approach. In W. Braud & R. Anderson (Eds.), *Transpersonal research methods for the social sciences: Honoring human experience* (pp. 69-94). Thousand Oaks, CA: Sage.

Anguccia, M. (2009).Children and war in Africa: The crisis continues in Northern Uganda. *International Journal on World Peace, 2*(1), 77-95. Retrieved from https://www.american.edu/cas/economics/ejournal/upload/Global_Majority_e_Journal_2-1_Beard.pdf

Arino, M.V. (2008). *Nepal: A gender view of the armed conflict and the peace agreement.* Retrieved from http://escolapau.uab.es/img/qcp/nepal_conflict_peace.pdf

Asian Human Rights Commission. (2013). *Nepal human rights in abeyance.* Retrieved from http://nepalconflictreport.ohchr.org/files/docs/2013-12-00_report_ahrc_eng.pdf

B. K., N. K. (2010). Maoist people's war and community adaptation. *Journal of Forest and Livelihood.* Retrieved from http://www.forestrynepal.org/images/publications/Maoist%20War%20and%20Adaptation.pdf

Betancourt, T. S., & Khan, K. T. (2008). The mental health of children affected by armed conflict: Protective processes and pathways to resilience. *International Review of Psychiatry, 20*(3), 317-328. doi:10.1080/09540260802090363

Bhattachan, K. B., & Webster, S. (2005). *Indigenous peoples, poverty reduction and conflict in Nepal.* Geneva, Switzerland: International Labour Organization. Retrieved from http://www.ilo.org/wcmsp5/groups/public/@ed_norm/@normes/documents/publication/wcms_100554.pdf

Bhattarai, B. R. (2003). The political economy of the people's war. In *The people's war in Nepal: Left perspectives.* New Delhi, India: Adroit Publishers.

Bishowkarma, D. R. (2010). *Caste based discrimination in schools: A study of Dalits in Ramechhap* (Unpublished MPhil dissertation). Kathmandu University School of Education: Dhulikhel, Nepal.

Blattman, C., Annan, J., Mazurana, D., & Carlson, K. (2010). *Civil war, reintegration, and gender in Northern Uganda.* Retrieved from http://www.chrisblattman.com/documents/research

/2010.CivilWarReintegrationGender.pdf

Bloomfield, D., Barnes, T., & Huyse, L. (Eds.). (2003). *Reconciliation after violent conflict: A handbook.* Stockholm, Sweden: Institute for Democracy and Electoral Assistance.

Boothby, N., Crawford, J., & Halperin, J. (2006). *Mozambique child soldier life outcome study: Lessons learned in rehabilitation and reintegration efforts.* Retrieved from http://childprotection.wikischolars.columbia.edu/file/view/Boothby+Crawford+%26+Halperin_Moza mbique+Child+Soldiers.pdf

Brett, R., McCallin, M., & O'Shea, R. (1996). *Children: The invisible soldiers.* Geneva, Switzerland: Quaker United Nations Office and International Catholic Child Bureau.

Burgress, R. (2009). Colombia's children at risk of recruitment into armed groups: Exploring a community-based, psychosocial pedagogy. *Journal of Education for International Development, 4*(1) 1-11.

Carspecken, P. F. (2001). Critical ethnography and education. In P. F. Carspecken & G. Walford (Eds.), *Critical ethnographies from Houston: Distinctive features and directions* (pp. 1-26). Londong, England: Emerald.

Catherine, H. A. (2008). *Protecting the rights of children in conflict with the law.* Geneva, Switzerland: University of Fribourg.

Center for Defense Information Colombia. (2001). *No safe haven from war.* Colombia: Author. Retrieved from www.yapi.org/publications/resourcepapers/ColHaven.pdf

Cohen, L., Manion, L., & Morrison, K. (2000). *Research methods in education* (5th ed.). London: Routledge.

Cohen, L., Manion, L., & Morrison, K. (2007). *Research methods in education* (6th ed.). London, England: Rutledge Falmer.

CRC Reporting Coalition. (2014). *Nepal civil society supplementary report on the convention on right of the child (CRC).* Kathmandu, Nepal: Author. Retrieved from http://tbinternet.ohchr.org/Treaties/CRC/Shared%20Documents/ NPL/INT_CRC_NGO_NPL_17964_E.pdf

Creswell, J. (2003). *Research design: Qualitative, quantitative and mixed methods.* Thousand Oaks, CA: Sage.

Creswell, J. W. (2007). *Qualitative inquiry and research design: Choosing among five approaches* (2nd ed.). Thousand Oaks, CA: Sage.

Creswell, J. W. (2012). *Educational research: Planning, conducting, and evaluating quantitative and qualitative research* (4th ed.). Boston, MA: Pearson.

Creswell, J. W. (2013). *Qualitative inquiry and research design: Choosing among five approaches* (3rd ed.). Thousand Oaks, CA: Sage.

Creswell, J.W. (2014). *Qualitative methods.* Retrieved from https://researchskillsgmm.files.wordpress.com/2014/10/research-design-creswell-chapter-9.pdf

Czyz, M. (2008). *Stopping the use of children soldiers: A global perspective.* Austria: European University Center for Peace Studies.

Dahal, D. R. (2002). Situation analysis of Dalits in Nepal. *National Dalit Strategy Report.* Kathmandu, Nepal: Action-Aid Nepal, CARE Nepal and Save the Children US. Retrieved from www.nepaldalitinfo.20m.com/ archives/Analysis2002.pdf

Dangal, M. R. (2010). *Aid effectiveness in basic and primary education in Nepal* (Unpublished doctoral thesis). Kathmandu University, Dhulikhel, Nepal.

Dawson, C. (2002). *Practical research methods: A user-friendly guide to mastering research.* United Kingdom: How To Books.

Denzin, N. K., & Lincoln, Y. S. (Eds.). (1994). *Handbook of qualitative research.* London, England: Sage.

Denzin, N. K., & Lincoln, Y. S. (2003). *The landscape of qualitative research: Theories and issues* (2nd ed.). Thousand Oaks, CA: Sage.

Devkota, S. P. (2014). *Ten years armed conflict and educational impact on children.* GRIN Verlag.

Devkota, S. P. (2015). Necessity of technical and vocational education for conflict affected. *The Journal of Training and Development, 1.* doi:10.3126/jtd.v1i0.13087

Dhungana, S. K. (2006). *Impact of conflict on service delivery in rural Nepal: The case of health sector.* Paper presented at the international Conference on Governance and Development, Kandy, Sri Lanka, 16-19 August 2006.

Do, Q. T., & Lyer, L. (2009). Mental health in the aftermath of conflict. In M. Garfinkel & S. Skaperdas (Eds.), *Oxford handbook of the economics of peace and conflict.* Retrieved from http://www.hbs.edu/faculty/Publication %20Files/10-040.pdf

Doek, J. (2011). The international legal framework for the protection in the armed conflict. *Disarmament Forum.* UNIDIR: Switzerland.

Farasat, W., & Hayner, P. (2009). *Country case study: Nepal.* Kathmandu, Nepal: International Center for Transitional Justice. Retrieved fromhttp://www.ictj.org/images/content/8/3/830.pdf

Feinstein International Centre. (2008). *Humanitarian agenda 2015: Nepal country case study.* Retrieved from http://fic.tufts.edu/assets/HA2015+Nepal+ Case+Study.pdf

Flick, U. (2006). *An introduction to qualitative research* (3rd ed.). London, England: Sage.

Flick, U. (2009). *An introduction to qualitative research* (4th ed.). New Delhi, India: Sage.

Folke, C. (2006). *Resilience: The emergence of a perspective for social–ecological systems analyses.* Retrieved from http://coastalcluster.curtin.edu.au/local/docs/Resilienc/Folke%202006_CS.pdf

Folke, C., Carpenter, S. R., Walker, B., Scheffer, M., Chapin, T., & Rockström, J. (2010). *Resilience thinking: Integrating resilience, adaptability and transformability.* Retrieved from http://www.stockholmresilience.org/

download/18.3e9bddec1373Daf16fa437/INsights_Transformations_111214-2.pdf

Forsther, M. P. (2011). *No work, no peace: Livelihoods of ex-combatants in Monrovia, Liberia.* Norway: University of Tromsø. Retrieved from http://munin.uit.no/bitstream/handle/10037/3687/thesis.pdf?sequence=2

Gautam, S. (2001). *Women and children in the periphery of the Maoists' people's war.* Kathmandu, Nepal: Institute of Human Rights Communication. Retrieved from http://nepalconflictreport.ohchr.org/files/docs/2001-12-00_report_ihricon_eng.pdf

Gautam, M. P. (2007). *Impact of armed conflict on children.* Retrieved from http://lup.lub.lu.se/luur/download?func=downloadFile&recordOId=1555327&fileOId=163622

Geven, L. M. (2008). *The Sage encyclopedia of qualitative research methods.* Thousand Oaks, CA: Sage.

Goldkuhl, G. (2012). *Pragmatism vs interpretivism in qualitative information systems research.* Sweden: Linköping University Electronic Press. Retrieved from http://liu.diva-portal.org/smash/get/diva2:515141/FULLTEXT01.pdf

Government of Nepal. (2007). *Interim constitution of Nepal 2007.* Kathmandu, Nepal: Author.

Gray, D. E. (2014). *Doing research in the real world.* Retrieved from http://www.amazon.com/Doing-Research-Real-World-David/dp/1446260194#reader_1446260194

Hart, J. (n.d.). *Children and armed conflict in Sri Lanka.* Colombo, Sri Lanka: Refugee Studies Center. Retrieved from http://www.rsc.ox.ac.uk/files/publications/other/dp-children-armed-conflict-sri-lanka.pdf

Hartley, J. (2004). Case study research. In C. Cassell & G. Symon (Eds.), *Essential guide to qualitative methods in organizational research* (pp. 323-333). London, England: Sage.

Harvey, R. (2001). *Children and armed conflict: A guide to international humanitarian and human rights law.* London, England: International Bureau of Children's Right.

Hogg, C. L. (2006, November). *Child recruitment in South Asian conflicts: A comparative analysis of Sri Lanka, Nepal and Bangladesh.* Retrieved from http://www.ciaonet.org.library3.webster.edu/wps/riia/0001545/0001545.pdf

Holloway, I. (1997). *Basic concepts for qualitative research.* London, England: Blackwell Science. Retrieved from http://fic.tufts.edu/assets/HA2015+Nepal+Case+Study.pdf

Human Rights Watch. (2007). *Hidden apartheid, shadow report for the UN Committee on the Elimination of Racial Discrimination (CERD).* Retrieved from http://chrgj.org/docs/IndiaCERDShadowReport.pdf

Human Rights Watch. (2014). *Silenced and forgotten: Survivors of Nepal's conflict-era sexual violence.* New York, NY: Author.

Informal Sector Service Center. (2007). *Nepal human rights year book 2006.*Kathmandu, Nepal: Informal Sector Service Centre.

International Committee of the Red Cross. (2009). *Families of missing persons in Nepal's study of their needs.* Kathmandu, Nepal: Author.

International Committee of Red Cross. (2011). *Children affected by armed conflict and other situation of violence.* Switzerland, Geneva: Author. Retrieved fromhttps://www.icrc.org/eng/assets/files/publications/icrc-002-4082.pdf

International Crisis Group. (2010). *War crimes in Sri Lanka.* Retrieved from http://www.crisisgroup.org/~/media/Files/asia/south-asia/srilanka / 191%20War%20Crimes%20in%20Sri%20Lanka.pdf

International Crisis Group. (2011). *Nepal: From two armies to one.*

Retrieved from http://www.crisisgroup.org/~/media/Files/asia/south-asia/ nepal/ 211%20Nepal%2z%20From%20Two%20Armies%20to%20One.pdf

International Dalit Solidarity Network. (2015). *Caste discrimination and human rights: A comprehensive compilation of how caste discrimination and similar forms of discrimination based on work and descent have been addressed by the UN treaty bodies, Universal Periodic Review, and the Special Procedures.* Denmark: Author. Retrieved from http://idsn.org/wpcontent/uploads/ 2015/08/UNcompilation2.pdf

International Human Right Clinic. (2013). *Assistance overdue: Ongoing needs of civilian affected of Nepal's armed conflict.* United States of America: Harvard Law School. Retrieved from http://hrp.law.harvard.edu/wp-content/uploads/2013/09/Nepal_Report_Online-2.pdf

Islam, F., & Uddyog, N. (2011). *Dalit women in Bangladesh: Multiple exclusions.* Bangladesh: Author. Retrieved from http://idsn.org/wp-content/uploads/ user_folder/pdf/New_files/Bangladesh/ Dalit_Women_in_Bangladesh_-_Multiple_Exclusions.pdf

International Youth Foundation. (2011). *Youth empowerment program evaluation: Executive version.* Baltimore: Author. Retrieved from http:/ /www.iyfnet.org/sites/default /files/MicrosoftYEP_Final_Report.pdf

Joshi, U., & Paudel, R. (2006).*Pilot research on internal displacement due to armed conflict in Dhanusha district.* Kathmandu, Nepal: National Human Rights Organization.

Kaplan, B., & Maxwell, J. A. (1994). *Qualitative research method for evaluating computer information system.* Thousand Oaks, CA: Sage.

Kershner, R., & Chaplain, R. (2001). *Understanding special educational needs – A teacher's guide to effective school-based research.* London, England: David Fulton.

Kumar, D., & Sharma, H. (2010). *Security sector reform in Nepal: Challenges and opportunities.* Kathmandu, Nepal: Friends for Peace.

Liebenberg, M., & Ungar, L. (2011). Assessing resilience across cultures using mixed methods: construction of the child and youth resilience measure. *Journal of Mixed Methods Research, 5,* 126-149. doi:10.1177/1558689811400607

Lincoln, Y. S., & Guba, E. G. (1985). *Naturalist inquiry.* Beverly Hills: Sage.

*Luitel, B. C., Settlemaier, E., & Taylor, P. C. (2011). Multi-paradigmatic transformative research as/for teacher education: An integral perspective.* In K. Tobin, B. Fraser, & C. McRobbie (Eds.), *International handbook of science education* (pp. 373-387). Dordrecht, The Netherlands: Springer.

Luthar, S. S., Cicchetti, D., & Becker, B. (2000). The construct of resilience: A critical evaluation and guidelines for future work. *Child Development, 71*(3). doi:10.1111/1467-8624.00164

Machel, G. (1996). *Promotion and protection of the rights of children: Impact of armed conflict on children.* Retrieved from http://daccess-ddsny.un.org/ doc/UNDOC/GEN/N96/219/55/PDF/N9621955.pdf?Open Element

Masten, A. (2011). *Resilience in children threatened by extreme adversity: Frameworks for research, practice, and translational synergy.* Retrieved from http://iom.nationalacademies.org/~/media/754155E6D97B4001A5FA9B1812A7CC44.ashx

Masten, A. (2012). *Risk and resilience in development.* Oxford, England: Oxford University Press.

Maxwell, J. A. (1996). *Qualitative research design: An interactive approach.* Thousand Oaks, CA: Sage.

McMillan, J. H., & Schumacher, S. (2001). *Research in education.* New York, NY: Harper Collins.

Miano, S. M. (2013). *Toward a child-oriented approach to reparations: Reflecting on the rights and needs of child affected of armed conflict.* Retrieved from http://fletcher.tufts.edu/Praxis/~/media/Fletcher/Microsites/praxis/xxviii/article2_miano_ChildReparations.pdf

Ministry of Peace and Reconstruction. (2011). *National action plan on implementation of the United Nations Security Council Resolutions*

*1325 & 1820.* Retrieved from http://www.gnwp.org/sites/default/files/resource-field_media/Nepal%20NAP.pdf

Ministry of Women, Children and Social Welfare. (2012). *National plan of action for children, Nepal.* Kathmandu. Retrieved from http://unicef.org.np/uploads/files/344006198179237619-npa-english-version-final.pdf

Moustaas, C. (1994). *Phenomenological research methods.* Thousand Oaks, CA: Sage.

National Institute for Policy Studies. (2013). *Nepal's peace agreement: A brief overview.* Kathmandu, Nepal: Author.

National Planning Commission. (2011). *Nepal peace and development strategy 2010-2015.* Kathmandu, Nepal: Author.

Ndulo, M. (2007).*Security, reconstruction, and reconciliation: When the wars end.* New York, NY: UCL Press.

Neely, H., & Tech, V. (2005). *Special education conflict management at the school building level: A multi-vocal synthesis.* Blacksburg, VA: Faculty of the Virginia Polytechnic Institute and State University.

Neupane, G. (2003). The Maoist movement in Nepal: A class perspective. In A. Karki & D. Seddon (Eds), *The people's war in Nepal: Left perspectives* (pp. 291–314). New Delhi, India: Adroit Publishers.

Nilsson, A. (2005). *Reintegrating ex-combatants in post-conflict societies.* Retrieved from http://www.pcr.uu.se/digitalAssets/67/67211_1sida4715en_ex_ combatants.pdf

Nübler, I. (1997). *Human resources development and utilization in demobilization and reintegration program.* Bonn, Germany: Bonn International Center for Conversion.

Nunan, D. (1993). *Research methods in language learning.* Cambridge, England: Cambridge University Press.

Onwuegbuzie, A. J., & Leech, N. L. (2007). Sampling designs in qualitative research: Making the sampling process more public. *The Qualitative Report, 12*(2), 238-254. Retrieved from http://www.nova.edu/ssss/QR/QR12-2/onwuegbuzie1.pdf

Opie, C. (2004). *Doing educational research.* New Delhi, India: Vistaar Publications.

Ozerdem, A., & Podder, S. (2011). Disarming youth combatants: mitigating youth radicalization and violent extremism. *Journal of Strategic Security, 4*(4), 63-80. Coventry, England: Coventry University.

Paardekooper, B. P. (2002). *Children of the forgotten war: A comparison of two intervention programmes for the promotion of well-being of Sudanese refugee children.* Amsterdam, Netherlands: Vrije Universiteit.

Paes, W. C. (2005). Eyewitness: The challenges of disarmament, demobilization and reintegration in Liberia. *International Peacekeeping, 12*(2), 253-61. Retrieve from http://core.ac.uk/download/pdf/17181282.pdf

Panta, P., & Nepal, S. (2003). *Status of children in Nepal: Population monograph of Nepal.* Kathmandu, Nepal: Central Bureau of Statistics.

Partnerships for Protecting Children in Armed Conflict. (2010). *Children affected by armed conflict in Nepal: Recommendations to the Security Council Working Group.* Retrieved from http://watchlist.org/wordpress/wp-content/uploads/WL-Briefing-Note-Nepal-20101.pdf

Pathak, B. (2005). *Politics of people's war and human rights in Nepal.* Kathmandu, Nepal: Bimipa Publication.

Patton, M. (1990). *Qualitative evaluation and research method* (2nd ed.). Newbury Park, CA: Sage Publication.

Pherali, T. J. (2011). *Education and conflict in Nepal: Possibilities for reconstruction.* Retrieved from http://www.informaworld.com/terms-and-conditions-of-access.pdf

Pradhan, A. (2012). *Sri Lanka's armed conflict: Children as affected and agents of peace.* Webster Groves, MO: Webster University. Retrieved from http://www.webster.ac.th/2012/pdf/thesis/2011-12/mair/Pradhan/Aditi%20Pradhan-%20Capstone%20Paper.pdf

Qayoom, F. (2014).Women and armed conflict: Widows in Kashmir. *International Journal of Sociology and Anthropology, 6*(5), 161-168. Retrieved from http://www.academicjournals.org/ebook/journal1398260481_IJSA%20Ebook-%20May%20-%202014%20issue.pdf

Reeves, T. C., &Hedberg, J. G. (2003). *Interactive learning systems evaluation.* Englewood Cliffs, NJ: Educational Technology Publications.

Richards, K. (2003). *Qualitative inquiry in TESOL.* New York, NY: Palgrave.

Saenz, M. M. (2012). *Reintegration of children associated with armed groups in Colombia.* Cambridge, MA: Harvard Graduate School of Education.

Sbovodova, V. (2013). *Impact of armed conflict on sexual violence against minors: Case study in South Kivu, Democratic Republic of Congo.* Retrieved from http://cdn.peaceopstraining.org/theses/svobodova.pdf

Sen, A. (1987). *The standard of living.* Cambridge, England: Cambridge University Press.

Sen, A. (1993).Capability and well-being. In M. Nussbaum & ASen (Eds.), *The quality of life*(pp. 30-53). Oxford, England: Clarendon Press.

Sen, A. (1995). Gender inequality and theories of justice. In M. Nussbaum & J. Glover (Eds.), *Women, culture and development: A study of human capabilities.* Oxford, England: Clarendon Press.

Sen, A. (1997). Maximization and the act of choice. *Econometrica, 65*(4), 745-779. Retrieved from http://web.pacuit.org/classes/rationality-fall2010/sen-max.pdf

Sen, A. (1999). *Development as freedom*. New York, NY: Knopf.

Shakya, A. (2006). *Social impact of armed conflict Nepal: Cause and impact.* Kathmandu, Nepal: Social Inclusion Research Fund.

Sharma, S. (2006). The Maoist movement: An evolutionary perspective. *Himalayan people's war: Nepal's Maoist rebellion* (pp. 38-57). New Delhi, India: Foundations Books.

Sokolowski, R. (2000). *Introduction to phenomenology*. Cambridge, England: Cambridge University Press.

Somasundaram, D. (2002). Child soldiers: Understanding the context. *British Medical Journal, 324*(7348), 1268–1271.Retrieved from http://resourcecentre. savethechildren.se/sites/default/files/documents/1268_0.pdf

Sook, K. H. (2003). *The types of speaking assessments tasks used by Korean Junior Secondary school English teachers.* Retrieved from http://www.asian-efl-journal.com/dec_03_gl.pdf

Spear, J. (2002). Disarmament and demobilization. In S. J. Stedman, D. Rothchild, & E. M. Cousens (Eds.), *Ending civil wars: The implementation of peace agreements* (pp. 189-203). London, England: Lynne Rienner Publishers.

Starks, H., & Trinidad, S. B. (2007). *Choose your method: A comparison of phenomenology, discourse analysis, and grounded theory.* Retrieved from http://www.tree4health.org/distancelearning/sites/www.tree4health.org.distancelearning/files/readings/Starks_Trinidad_choosing_qual_approach_article.pdf

Taylor, P. C., & Wallace, J. (2007). *Qualitative research in postmodern times.* Amsterdam, Netherlands: Springer.

The Government of Nepal. (2012). *The optional protocol to the convention on the rights of the child on the involvement of children in armed conflict.* Nepal. Retrieved from https://www.google.com.np/url?...111396085,d.c2E&cad=rja

The United Nations Children's Fund. (2003). *Guide to the optional protocol on the involvement of children in armed conflict.* Retrieved from http://www.unicef.org/sowc06/pdfs/option_protocol_conflict.pdf

United Nations. (2013). *The six grave violations against children during armed conflict: The Legal Foundation.* Retrieved from https://childrenandarmedconflict.un.org/publications/WorkingPaper-1_SixGraveViolationsLegalFoundation.pdf

United Nations Development Program. (2010). *Country program action plan between the governments of Tajikistan and the United Nations development program*

*2010-2015*. Retrieved from http://www.undp.org/content/dam/ tajikistan/docs/legal_framework/UNDP_TJK_CPAP_2010-2015_eng.pdf

United Nations Development Program. (2014). *Completing Nepal's transition: Reflections on Nepal's peace agreement*. Kathmandu, Nepal: Author.

United Nations Office of the High Commissioner for Human Rights. (2012). *Nepal conflict report: Executive summary.* Switzerland, Geneva: Author. Retrieved fromhttp://www.ohchr.org/Documents/Countries/NP/OHCHR_ExecSumm_Nepal_Conflict_report2012.pdf

United Nations. (1999). *Disarmament, demobilization and reintegration of ex- combatants in a peacekeeping environment. Principles and guidelines.* New York, NY: Author.

Upreti, B. R. (2004). *The price of neglect: From resource conflict to Maoist insurgency in the Himalayan kingdom.* Kathmandu, Nepal: Bhrikuti.

Upreti, B. R. (2005a). Conflict transformation and peace building: Choices of approaches and strategies for Nepal. *Readings on Governance and Development, 5*, 24-33.

Upreti, B. R. (2005b). *Human rights approach to conflict transformation ensuring respect and fulfillment of human rights in peaceful settlement of the armed conflict in Nepal.* A paper presented at Human Rights and Peace Conference organized by National Human Rights Commission in Kathmandu on 24–25 January 2005.

Upreti, B. R. (2006). *Armed conflict and peace agreement in Nepal: The Maoists insurgency, past negotiations and opportunities for conflict transformation.* New Delhi, India: Adroit Publishers.

Upreti, B. R. (2008). *Framework for management of post-conflict transition in Nepal: Some issues and concerns.* A paper presented at the national seminar on Democracy and Post-conflict Management in Nepal, Nepal Foundation for Advance Studies, Kathmandu, Nepal.

Upreti, B. R. (2009). *Nepal from war to peace: Legacies of the past and hopes for the future.* New Delhi, India: Adroit Publishers.

Upreti, B. R., & Boker, U. M. (2010). *Livelihood insecurity and social conflict in Nepal.* Kathmandu: National Centre of Competence in Research. Retrieved from http://www.dsgz.geo.uzh.ch/pdfs/Upreti_Livelihoods.pdf

Van Maanen, M. (1990). *Researching lived experience: Human science for an action sensitive pedagogy.* London, England: The Alehouse Press.

Verhey, B. (2002). *Child soldiers: Prevention, demobilization and reintegration* (Dissemination Notes). Washington, DC: Conflict Prevention and Reconstruction Unit, World Bank.

Walker, B., & Salt, D. (2006). *Resilience thinking: Sustaining ecosystems and people in a changing world.* Washington, DC: Island Press.

Walsham, G. (2005). Learning about being critical. *Information Systems Journal, 15*(2), 111–117. doi:10.1111/j.1365-2575.2004.00189.x

Watch List on Children and Armed Conflict. (2005). *Caught in the middle: Mounting violations against children in Nepal's armed conflict.* Kathmandu, Nepal: Author. Retrieved from http://www.watchlist.org/reports/pdf/ nepal.report.20050120.pdf

Watson, C. (2009). *Socio-economic reintegration of ex-combatants: What role for the European Union*? Background paper produced for a roundtable discussion. Brussels. Retrieved from http://www.international-alert.org/sites/default/ files/publications/ Economic_Reintegration_march_2010.pdf

Wessells, M. G. (1998). Children, armed conflict, and peace- review essay. *Journal of Peace Research, 35*(5), 635-646. doi:10.1177/0022343398035005006

Willis, J. W. (2007). *Foundations of qualitative research: Interpretive and critical approaches.* Thousand Oaks, CA: Sage.

Yin, R. K. (2003). *Case study research: Design and methods* (3rd ed.). Thousand Oaks, CA: Sage.

Yin, R. K. (2014). *Case study research: Designs and methods* (3rd ed.). Thousand Oaks, CA: Sage.

# Appendix-I

(Opted, Selected and Practised)

Interview Themes

1. Background
   a. Your name, schooling (grade, subjects of interest, likes/dislikes) , teachers, friends, neighbourhood and cooperation in education
   b. Family enemy
   c. Family, parents profession, their social prestige and relation
   d. Parents' pereception on educaiton, contributation on education,
   e. Family economic condition
   f. Ethinicity/caste and cultural practice by ethicinity/caste in relation 10 year period
   g. Local politcal personnel's role in education
   h. Social discrimination
   i. Gender issues
   j. Acedmic perfermence
2. Internal environment of learning
   a. Class regularity

b. Fearful environment

c. Teacher devotion in students' learning

d. Security situation

3. External envoronment of learning

a. Media update

b. Peer support

c. Local support

d. Neighbourhood support

e. Development partners' support

k. Their feeling of secureness and threats

4. Experience about conflict

a. migration,

b. hard time,

c. family lost,

d. self injured,

e. self envolvement

5. Adversities after peace agreement

a. Family response at present

b. Local society response

c. Social behaviour/threats and its link to education (benefits, disadvantage)

d. Development patner response

e. Government respose

f. Continuity on education

g. Present feeling with/without education (advantage, disadvantage)

h. Adverse/ good situation caused by education level
i. Social prestige/ unprestige by education
j. Continueity in eduation or job
k. Feeling about present occupation
l. Work in partnership/ job situation
m. Problems faced in job/professional or educational life
n. Family support and your experience
o. Societal support (Peace committee) and experience
p. Local people support and experience
q. Development patner support and experience
r. Government support and experience
s. Revel party support and experience
t. Expection and its fulfillment

# Index

## D

## E



## F



## G



## H

## M



## N



## O



## P

## T